攀 登 长 城 证 明 书

Certificate to show that you have climbed the Great Wall of China

世 界 文 化 遗 产
World Cultural Heritage

不到长城非好汉

NOT A PLUCKY HERO UNTIL ONE REACHES THE GREAT WALL

_____攀登万里长城，特此证明。

This is to certify that _____*has climbed the Great Wall of China.*

日期 Date：_____

The Great Wall

长　城

만 리 장 성
Die Große Mauer
La Grande Muraille
La Gran Muralla
Grande Muraglia
Великая китайская стена

外 文 出 版 社

前 言

长城是中国古代的军事防御设施。在中国辽阔的土地上，长城东西横贯、绵延数万里，东起辽宁的鸭绿江畔，一路翻山越岭、穿跨沙漠荒原，奔向莽莽雪山。

长城从公元前 7 世纪春秋战国至公元 17 世纪的明代末年，它的修建延续了 2000 多年。先后有 20 多个王朝修筑过长城。其中工程最大的是秦始皇修筑的秦长城，汉武帝修筑的汉长城和明太祖修筑的明长城。

长城已经成为中华民族精神的象征，它的坚强不屈激励着中华儿女战胜一切困难，勇往直前。长城作为防御入侵的军事设施，证明了中华民族自古以来热爱和平、反对入侵的坚定信念和不懈追求。

长城是中华历史悠久的丰碑和文化的宝藏。长城在两千多年的封建社会兴衰中，经历了无数金戈铁马、血雨腥风、群雄逐鹿、叱咤风云的历史。同时，沿长城内外，在游牧文化和农耕文化的冲撞交融中，也产生、发展和保存了大量最珍贵的文化遗存。

1987 年，长城被联合国科教文组织列入世界文化遗产名录。长城是中华瑰宝，早在几百年前即被列入中古世界七大奇迹之一。只有一个伟大的民族，才能建造起这样一座伟大的长城。

Foreword（英文）

An important military fortification in ancient times, the Great Wall runs thousands of kilometers on the vast territory of China. From the Yalu River in Liaoning Province, it snakes westward across mountains, deserts and snow-covered plateaus.

The construction of the wall lasted more than 2,000 years -- from the 7th century BC during the Spring and Autumn Period to the 17th century AD, during the late Ming Dynasty. Over 20 dynasties contributed to its construction. The three most important construction projects were respectively carried out during the reigns of the First Emperor of the Qin Dynasty, Emperor Wudi of the Han Dynasty and Emperor Taizu of the Ming Dynasty.

The Great Wall has become a symbol of the Chinese nation, representing its persistence and bravery. As a defense work, it shows the Chinese people's love of peace and determination to repel foreign invasions.

The Great Wall has long been deemed a historical monument and a cultural treasure of China. Throughout history it witnessed chaos and conflicts amidst warring feudal dynasties. Meanwhile, the blending between nomadic and agricultural civilizations inside and outside the Great Wall has produced a number of cultural relics of historic importance.

In 1987, the Great Wall was put on the World Cultural Heritage list by UNESCO. But hundreds of years earlier, it had been reputed as one of the Seven Wonders of the World. Only a great nation could have made such a great monument.

前書き（日文）

　長城は古代中国の軍事防御施設である。東は遼寧省の鴨緑江口から、西は中国の西北に聳え立つ高い雪山に至るまで、山川や広漠を越え、えんえんと数万華里に及んで走っている。

　長城の構築は、西暦前7世紀の春秋戦国時代から西暦17世紀の明代末年に至ゐまでの、2000年あまりの長い歳月が続いた。前後には合わせて20以上の王朝が長城を構築したことがある。このうち、秦の始皇帝が築造した秦長城、漢の武帝が構築した漢長城と明の太祖が築造した明長城は、工事がもっとも雄大である。

　長城はすでに中華民族の不屈精神のシンボルとなっており、困難に打ち勝ち勇敢に前へ進むよう中華子女をいつまでも励ましている。長城は侵略を防ぐための軍事防御施設であり、平和を熱愛し、侵略に反対する中華民族の昔からの信念とそれを求める証拠である。

　長城は凝集された中華民族の悠久な歴史と文化の宝である。2000年以上つづいた封建社会の中、長城幾たびも戦乱に見舞われたにもかかわらず、遊牧文化と農耕文化と融けあいながら、夥しい量の珍しい文化財を残してきた。

　1987年、長城は国連ユネスコにより名が「世界遺産リスト」に登録されるようになった。長城は中華民族の輝かしい宝として、早くも数100年前に「中古世界七大奇跡の一つ」に指定された。偉大な民族でなければこんな雄大な長城を築造することがでないはずである。

서언（韓文）

　장성은 중국 고대의 군사 방어시설로 중국 넓은 국토의 동서를 관통하여 수만리에 달한다. 장성은 동쪽 요녕성의 압록강변부터 산을 넘고 영을 건너 황망한 사막을 지나 망망한 설산까지 이른다.

　장성은 기원전 7 세기의 춘추·전국시기부터 17 세기 명나라말년까지 수건하였는데 2000 여 년의 시간이 지속되었다. 선후하여 20 여 개 왕조에서 장성을 수건하였다. 그 중 공정이 가장 큰 것은 진시황이 수건한 진장성, 한무제가 수건한 한장성, 명태조가 수건한 명장성이다.

　장성은 중화민족정신의 상징이다. 장성의 견고하구 굽어들지 않는 성질은 중화의 아들딸들이 모든 곤난을 극복하고 용감무쌍하게 앞으로 전진하게 격려한다. 장성은 외래의 침입을 방어하는 군사시설로서 중화민족이 자고이래 평화를 사랑하고 침략을 반대하는 견의한 심념과 끝임없는 추구를 증명한다.

　장성은 중국역사의 불후한 걸작이며 문화적 보물이다. 장성은 2000 여 년간의 중국 봉건사회의 흥망 속에서 무수한 전란과 여러 조대의 교체를 경과하였다. 동시, 장성 내외의 유목문화와 농업문화의 충돌과 융합 과정에서 많은 진귀한 문화유산을 발생·발전·　보존하였다.

　1987 년, 장성은 유네스코로부터 세계문화유산명록에 기록되었다. 장성은 중화민족의 진귀한 보물로서 몇백년 전에 이미 세계 7 대 불가사의 중의 하나로 되었다. 오직 위대한 민족만이 위대한 장성을 건축할 수 있는 것이다.

Avant-propos（法文）

　La Grande Muraille était le gigantesque ouvrage de défense militaire de la Chine antique. Partant du bord du fleuve Yalujiang dans la province du Liaoning, elle s'étire d'est en ouest sur plus de 5 000 kilomètres dans le vaste territoire de Chine, en franchissant montagnes et vaux, traversant déserts et steppes immenses et se prolongeant à travers montagnes enneigées.

　La construction de la Grande Muraille dura plus de 2 000 ans de l'époque des Automnes et Printemps et des Royaumes combattants du VIIe siècle avant Jésus-Christ à la fin de la dynastie des Ming du XVIIe siècle. Plus de 20 dynasties entreprirent des travaux dont les plus importants ont été marqués par la Grande Muraille des Qin (221 – 207 av. J.-C.), construite sous le règne de l'empereur Shihuangdi, celle des Han (206 av. J.-C. – 220), réalisée sous le règne de l'empereur Wudi, et celle des Ming (1368 – 1644), achevée sous le règne de l'empereur Taizu.

　La Grande Muraille est déjà devenue le symbole de l'esprit de la nation chinoise. Sa solidité à toute épreuve encourage les Chinois à surmonter toutes les difficultés et à aller hardiment de l'avant. En tant qu'ouvrage de défense militaire, la Grande Muraille témoigne des convictions inébranlables et de l'aspiration soutenue de la nation chinoise qui est depuis toujours éprise de paix et qui s'oppose fermement à l'invasion.

　La Grande Muraille est le monument de la longue histoire de la Chine et un trésor culturel. Durant plus de 2 000 ans de prospérité et de décadence de la société féodale, la Grande Muraille connut une histoire caractérisée par les guerres sanglantes, les luttes pour la suprématie et l'héroïsme sublime. L'antagonisme et les échanges entre la culture nomade et la culture agricole des deux côtés de la Grande Muraille, et leur fusion ont engendré des cultures de nouveau type qui nous ont laissé de nombreux sites précieux.

　En 1987, la Grande Muraille a été inscrite sur la Liste du Patrimoine mondial par l'UNESCO. Trésor de la Chine, elle figure depuis plusieurs siècles parmi les Sept Merveilles médiévales du monde. Seule une grande nation a pu bâtir une telle Grande Muraille.

Vorwort（德文）

　Die Große Mauer ist eine antike Verteidiungsanlage Chinas. Mit einer Länge von mehreren Zehntausenden Kilometern windet sie sich auf und ab über die Bergketten Nordchinas, vom Yalu-Fluss im Osten bis zum Jiayuguan-Pass im Westen.

　Die Bauarbeiten an diesem imposanten Bauwerk begonnen in der Frühlings- und Herbstperiode und in der Zeit der Streitenden Reiche (um das 7. Jh. v. Chr.) und endeten am Ende der Ming-Dynastie (um das 17. Jh.). Im Verlaufe von mehr als 2000 Jahren nahmen insgesamt über 20 Dynastien an ihren Bauarbeiten teil. Zu ihrem größten Bauprojekt gehörten die Große Mauer der Qin, die auf Befehl von dem ersten Qin-Kaiser Ying Zhong gebaute wurde, die Große Mauer der Han und der Ming, die jeweils auf Anweisung von dem Han-Kaiser Wu Di und von dem Ming-Kaiser Tai Zu errichtet wurden.

　Die Große Mauer ist das Symbol des Geistes der chinesischen Nation, alle Schwierigkeiten zu überwinden und mutig vorwärtszuschreiten. Als eine Verteidigungsanlage beweist die Große Mauer, dass sich die chinesische Nation von alters her anstrengt, den Frieden zu lieben und gegen Invasionen zu kämpfen.

　Die Große Mauer gilt als ein monumentales Werk der langen Geschichte und auch als eine Schatzkammer der chinesischen Nation. Im Verlaufe der Jahrhunderte schufen die innerhalb und außerhalb der Großen Mauer anlässigen Hirten und Bauern gemeinsam eine glänzende Kultur und hinterließen hier viele historische Denkmäler.

　Heute ist die Große Mauer eine große touristische Attraktion und ein Zeugni santiker chinesischer Baukunst. Im Jahre 1987 wurde sie von der UNESCO in die „Liste des Weltkultur- und Naturerbes" aufgenommen.

慕田峪长城
The Mutianyu Great Wall
慕田峪長城
무톈위장성
La Grande Muraille de Mutianyu
Die Große Mauer bei Mutianyu
La Grande Muraglia di Mutianyu
Участок Мутяньюй
La Gran Muralla de Mutianyu

Prólogo（西文）

La Gran Muralla China, obra monumental que en la antigüedad funcionó como bastión de defensa militar, atraviesa el vasto territorio del país, extendiéndose por miles de kilómetros que parten desde la orilla del río Yalujiang, en la provincia de Liaoning, en el este, y terminan entre las montañas nevadas del oeste.

Más de 2.000 años duró la construcción de este baluarte, cuyas obras se iniciaron en el Período de la Primavera y Otoño del siglo VII (a.n.e.) y terminaron en las postrimerías de la dinastía Ming, en el siglo XVII. Una veintena de dinastías chinas se empeñaron en la edificación de tan colosal obra, entre las que jugaron un papel destacado monarcas entusiastas como el primer emperador de la dinastía Qin, el emperador Wudi de la dinastía Han y el Taizu de la dinastía Ming, quienes nos legaron la Gran Muralla de Qin, Han y Ming, respectivamente.

Con el paso del tiempo, la fortificación devino símbolo espiritual de la nación china y su firmeza y fortaleza animan a los habitantes de este país a vencer las dificultades y marchar adelante. Su carácter defensivo demuestra además, la aspiración invariable del pueblo chino por la paz y su firme resistencia contra las invasiones.

La obra es también un monumento a la larga historia china y depósito de cuantiosos tesoros culturales. Durante sus más de 2 mil años de historia, a lo largo de ella se han encontrado numerosas reliquias generadas y desarrolladas por los conflictos e intercambios entre la civilización ganadera y la agrícola.

En 1987, la UNESCO (Organización de las Naciones Unidas para la Educación, la Ciencia y la Cultura) incluyó en su lista de Patrimonio Cultural de la Humanidad a la Gran Muralla, joya arquitectónica que desde hace centenares de años es considerada una de las Siete Maravillas de la Arquitectura Moderna.

Предисловие（俄文）

Великая китайская стена была в древности комплексной системой обороны. Она протянулась на 5660 км с востока, с берега реки Ялуцзян на запад в северном Китае.

Строительство Стены началось в VII веке до н.э. в эпоху Воюющих царств, и закончилось в конце династии Мин 17-ого века. Это продолжалось на более 2000 лет. Всего более 20 династий строили Великую стену. Особенно при династиях Цинь (221 до н.э. – 206 до н.э.), Хань (206 до н.э. – 220) и Мин (1368 – 1644), длина Стены – больше десяти тысяч ли (ли – 500 м) .

Великая китайская стена является символом древнекитайской цивилизации, воплощением мудрости древних китайцев. Великая стена доказывает то, что китайский народ с давних времен любит мир, противодействует нашествию.

Великая стена – сокровище китайской культуры и памятник китайской истории. В течение более 2000 лет Великая стена страдает много. Между тем, за и внутри Великой стеной родилось и сохранилось большое количество культурных достопримечательностей.

В 1987 г. Великая китайская стена была занесена в реестр объектов мирового культурного наследия. Ста лет назад она уже вошла в семь чудес древнего мира.

Premessa（意大利文）

La Grande Muraglia, antica struttura di difesa militare della Cina, serpeggia nell'immenso territorio cinese estendosi da oriente, lungo le rive del fiume Yalu, nell'attuale provincia del Liaoning, fino ad occidente, lungo le cime dei monti innevati di Qilian delle province attuali del Gansu e del Qinghai, per una lunghezza totale di circa 6.300 chilometri.

Fu edificata a partire dal 700 a.C., durante il Regno di Chu e fu terminata 2.000 anni dopo, in epoca Ming. Furono più di 20 principi di regni e dinastie feudali che contribuirono alla sua costruzione, al suo restauro ed al suo miglioramento; in particolar modo durante le dinastie Qin, Han e Ming. La maggior parte della Grande Muraglia fu costruita su montagna e vallate, come un gigantesco drago, simbolo della nazione cinese, che vola e salta da picco a picco.

Essa costituisce un importante significato per il popolo cinese, per incoraggiarlo a superare le difficoltà e andare sempre avanti.

La Grande Muraglia è il monumento più rappresentativo della lunga storia della nazione cinese e dei suoi tesori culturali, giacché vide il susseguirsi delle vicissitudini avvenute nel corso di 2.000 anni di storia e assistette ai cambiamenti e agli scontri avvenuti nel corso dei secoli fra le civiltà nomadi e agricole, fungendo da barriera protettiva di importanti patrimoni culturali.

Nel 1987 fu inserita nella lista di patrimoni culturali mondiali dell'UNESCO.

长城－北京地区

　　北京位于华北平原的北端，其西部和北部的燕山山脉、太行山像一道天然屏障，阻隔在华北平原和内蒙古高原之间。其间经河流的长期冲刷和自然风华侵蚀，在崇山峻岭间形成了许多峡谷隘口，成为南北的重要通道。北京地区的长城就是依据"因险制塞"的原则修建的，这些通道隘口修成了长城的关口，而蜿蜒的长城则依着山势起伏而连接各关口，形成险要的防御系统。

　　北京地区的长城经历了漫长的发展过程，从战国七雄之一的燕开始修筑，经秦、汉、魏、晋、北齐、北周、隋、唐等朝的更迭，直到明朝。明朝先后派大将徐达、戚继光、谭纶镇守、修筑长城，由于明朝迁都北京，故这一地区的长城修筑的十分坚固，成为万里长城中最精华的部分，据测量，北京地区长城共长629公里，从平谷入境，经怀柔、密云、昌平、延庆、门头沟六个区县，呈半环状分布于北部山区。

八达岭长城
The Badaling Great Wall
八達嶺長城
바다링장성
La Grande Muraille de Badaling
Die Große Mauer bei Badaling
La Grande Muraglia di Badaling
Участок Бадалин
La Gran Muralla de Badaling, en Beijing

The Great Wall in the Beijing Area （英文）

　　The city of Beijing lies in the northernmost part of the North China Plain. Embracing the city in the west and north, the Yanshan and Taihang mountains protect the North China Plain from the Inner Mongolia Plateau. For millions of years, water and wind erosion has gouged many valleys and gorges amidst the rolling mountains, which later served as important passages linking north and south in ancient times. The Great Wall near Beijing was constructed so as to block these passages, forming a military fortification system.

　　The construction of the Beijing section began in the time of the State of Yan, one of the seven powers during the Warring States Period (475-221BC), and continued until the Ming Dynasty, through the Qin, Han, Wei, Jin, Northern Qi, Northern Zhou, Sui and Tang dynasties. The Ming court dispatched such famous generals as Xu Da and Qi Jiguang to reinforce and defend the Great Wall. After the Ming Dynasty relocated its capital to Beijing, the Great Wall was further consolidated. A survey indicates that the Great Wall stretches for 629 kilometers in the Beijing area, across six counties and districts—Pinggu, Huairou, Miyun, Changping, Yanqing and Mentougou. The wall describes a rough semi-circle in the mountainous areas of northern Beijing.

北京地域の長城（日文）

　北京は華北平原の北端にあり、その西部と北部を走る燕山山脈と太行山脈は、あたかも天然の障壁のように、華北平原と蒙古高原とを遮っている。長年にわたる風雨の浸食を受け、山々の間に形成されたさまざまな峡谷や峠は、南北を行き来する大切な通路となった。北京地域の長城は、「険を要塞にする」原則に踏まえて構築したもので、険阻な山々の上に構築した蛇行する城壁は、各関所を一体に連ねて、完全な防御システムをつくりあげた。

　北京地域の長城はかなり長い発展の道をたどってきた。築造は「七雄」の一つの燕（えん）からはじまり、秦、漢、魏、晋、北斉、北周、隋、唐などを経て明に至った。明代は長城を築造するために、前後にして大将軍徐達、戚継光、譚綸らを監督将軍として指名した。明が都を北京に遷す計画に合わせ、北京地域の長城はひときわ堅固なようにつくられ、万里の長城の中においてももっともすばらしい区間となっている。測定によれば、北京地域の長城はあわせて６２９ｋｍのものがあり、平谷から北京いりして懐柔、密雲、昌平、延慶と門頭溝の山間地帯を、三日月形を呈してうねうねと走っている。

幕田峪长城
The Mutianyu Great Wall
慕田峪長城
무텐위장성
La Grande Muraille de Mutianyu
Die Große Mauer bei Mutianyu
La sezione della Grande Muraglia di Mutianyu
Участок Мутяньюй
La Gran Muralla de Mutianyu

베이징 지역 장성（韩文）

　베이징은 화베이 평원의 북쪽에 위치해 있으며 장성의 서쪽과 북쪽에 위치한 옌산산맥, 타이항산은 하나의 천연적인 병풍을 이루어 화베이평원과 네이멍구고원을 갈라놓고 있다. 긴 세월동안 강물의 침식과 자연 풍화작용은 높은 산령 사이에 많은 협곡을 형성했으며 남북을 이어놓는 중요한 통로로 되었다. 베이징 지역의 장성은 "험요한 곳에 요새를 구축하는" 원칙에 근거하여 수건하였는데 이런 교통 요충지를 이용하여 장성에 관문을 구축하였으며 구불구불한 장성은 산세에 따라 여러 관문을 연결하여 험준한 방어 시스템을 형성하였다.

　베이징 지역의 장성은 오랜 발전과정을 경과하였다. 전국칠웅(戰國七雄)의 하나인 연(燕)나라 시기부터 시작하여 진(秦), 한(漢), 위(魏), 진(晋), 북제(北齊), 북주(北周), 수(隋), 당(唐) 등 시대의 교체를 경과하여 명나라 시기까지 구축하였다.

La Grande Muraille dans la région de Beijing（法文）

Beijing se situe à l'extrémité nord de la plaine de la Chine du Nord. La chaîne de montagnes Yanshan et celle Taihang à l'ouest et au nord de Beijing ondulent comme une barrière naturelle entre la plaine de la Chine du Nord et le plateau de la Mongolie intérieure. Sous l'érosion fluviale et l'action des intempéries pendant une longue durée, nombre de défilés et de cols se formèrent dans les montagnes et devinrent d'importants passages allant du sud au nord. La Grande Muraille de la région de Beijing fut construite selon le principe de "mise en place des forteresses sur les positions stratégiques". Ainsi, ces passages et cols ont été aménagés en passes, reliée entre elles par la Grande Muraille qui serpente sur les crêtes des montagnes, formant un système de défense difficile d'accès.

La Grande Muraille de la région de Beijing connut une longue période de construction depuis les Yan, un des sept Etats puissants de l'époque des Royaumes combattants, jusqu'à la dynastie des Ming en passant par les Qin, les Han, les Wei, les Jin, les Qi du Nord, les Zhou du Nord, les Sui, les Tang et d'autres. La cour des Ming envoya successivement les fameux généraux Xu Da, Qi Jiguang et Tan Lun en garnison sur place et diriger la construction de la Grande Muraille. Comme la dynastie des Ming transféra sa capitale à Beijing, la Grande Muraille de la région de Beijing est très solide et la plus belle de l'ensemble. La Grande Muraille s'étire sur 629 kilomètres dans la région de Beijing en traçant un demi-cercle dans les montagnes du nord à Pinggu, Huairou, Miyun, Changping, Yanqing et Mentougou.

司马台长城
The Simatai Great Wall.
司馬台長城
쓰마타이장성
La Grande Muraille de Simatai
Der Mauerabschnitt Simatai
La sezione della Grande Muraglia di Simatai
Участок Великой Китайской стены Сыматай
La Gran Muralla de Simatai

Die Große Mauer in der Umgebung Beijings（德文）

Beijing liegt am nördlichen Rand der nordchinesischen Ebene. Im Westen und Norden ragen die Gebirge Yanshan und Taihang empor. Diese beiden Gebirgsketten bilden einen natürlichen Schutzwall wischen der nordchinesischen Ebene und dem Plateau der Inneren Mongolei. Im Verlaufe der Jahrtausende entstanden durch Flusserosionen in diesen Gebirgsgebieten viele Schluchten und Pässe, die wichtige Durchgänge zwischen Süden und Norden bildeten. Die Große Mauer in der Umgebung Beijings wurde entsprechend den örtlichen geografischen Verhältnissen gebaut: Die Festungen wurden in den Schluchten und an den Pässen errichte, die durch die auf dem Bergrücken gebauten Mauerabschnitte miteinander verbunden sind.

Die Große Mauer in der Umgebung Beijings wurde zuerst von dem Yan-Reich während der Zeit der Streitenden Reiche gebaut. Die Bauarbeiten wurden in der Qin-, der Han-, der Wei-, der Jin-, der Nördlichen Qi- un der Nördlichen Zhou-, der Sui-, der Tang- und der Ming-Dynastie fortgesetzt. Die Große Mauer der Ming-Zeit wurde unter der Leitung der Generale Xu Da, Qi Jiguang und Tan Lun gebaut und ist bis heute im großen und ganzen gut erhalten. Untersuchungen beweisen, dass es in der Umgebung Beijings sechs Mauerabschnitte mit einer gesamten Länge von 629 km gibt. Sie erstrecken sich von Pingu aus durch Huairou, Miyun, Changping und Yanqing bis nach Mentougou.

La Gran Muralla en Beijing （西文）

Beijing ocupa el extremo septentrional de la planicie de Huabei. Al oeste y norte de la ciudad pasan las cordilleras Yanshan y Taihangshan, en ese orden, extendidas como barrera natural entre la llanura de Huabei y la meseta mongola. Entre los picos y montañas, debido al derrubio del agua y el viento, aparecieron muchos valles que formaban pasos importantes para conectar el norte y el sur del país. Los diseñadores de la Gran Muralla, al pasar por Beijing, aprovecharon plenamente estas condiciones del terreno y construyeron fuertes castillos militares conectados por los muros levantados en las montañas, formando un complejo defensivo.

La edificación del bastión en la región de Beijing se inició en la época del Estado Yan, durante los Estados Combatientes, y continuó a lo largo de dinastías posteriores, como Qin, Han, Wei, Jin, Qi del Norte, Zhou del Norte, Sui, Tang y Ming. Los emperadores de esta última ordenaron a los generales Xu Da, Qi Jiguang y Tan Dun asumir los trabajos de terminación de la obra y su ocupación.

Después que la capital de la dinastía Ming se trasladó de Nanjing a Beijing, la Gran Muralla, por su cercanía a la ciudad, fue especialmente reforzada en sus proximidades, que constituyen sus partes más esenciales. Se calcula que la fortaleza abarca 629 Km. dentro del territorio de la provincia, a donde entra por el distrito de Pinggu, para atravesar luego los de Huairou, Miyun, Changping, Yanqing y Mentougou, presentando forma de semicírculo en la zona montañosa del norte de la ciudad.

Le sezioni di muraglia nell'area di Pechino （意大利文）

Pechino è situata nella parte settentrionale della pianura Huabei, nella Cina settentrionale. Le catene Yanshan e Taihang che contornano Pechino a ovest e a nord fungono da paravento naturale, isolando la pianura Huabei dall'altopiano della Mongolia Interna. Le correnti d'acqua e l'erosione del vento hanno portato nel periodo alla formazione fra le alte creste e le montagne torreggiante numerose gole, valle e valichi. La muraglia si snoda fra le vette e costituisce un sistema difensivo dalla posizione strategica.

Le sezioni di Grande Muraglia dell'area circostante Pechino furono edificate seguendo l'andamento ondulato naturale delle cime su cui si ergono.

L'opera di costruzione della muraglia intorno a Pechino fu avviata durante il regno Yan del Periodo degli Stati Combattenti, e fu completata all'epoca della dinastia Ming; furono i principi Qin, Han, Wei, Jin, Beiqi, Beizhou, Sui e Tang che contribuirono alla sua costruzione ed alle diverse fasi di restauro a cui furono sottoposte. Durante la dinastia Ming l'imperatore incaricò i Xu Da e Qi Jiguang di migliorare quest'opera difensiva. Poiché all'epoca della dinastia Ming la capitale fu trasferita a Pechino, le sezioni di muraglia circostanti furono rafforzate e in diverse parti edificate a nuovo in uno stile architettonico caratteristico e ancora oggi ben conservato. Dai misuramenti effettuati le sezioni di Grande Muraglia nell'area circostante Pechino si estendono per 629 chilometri attraverso i sei distretti di Pinggu, Huairou, Miyun, Changping, Yanqing e Mentougou.

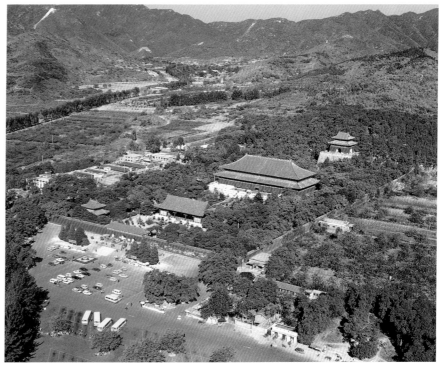

Участок Великой стены в Пекине （俄文）

Пекин расположен на севере равнины Хуабэй. Гора Яньшань на западе и гора Тайханшань на севере отделяют равнину Хуабэй от нагорья внутренней Монголии. Ущелья и горные перевалы, формирующиеся от плескания реки и выветривания стали важными проходами. При строительстве участка Великой стены в Пекине они стали проходами стены. Стена, протянувшаяся через горы, соединяет проходы вместе. Таким образом, формировалась неприступная система обороны.

Строительство участка Великой стены в Пекине продолжалось много лет. Царство Янь в эпоху Воюющих царств первым начало строить стену, потом династии Цин, Хань, Вэй, Цзинь, Бэйци, Бэйчжоу, Суй, Тань и другие продолжили строительство. В династии Мин генералы Суй Да, Ци Цзигуань и Тань Лун поочередно были назначены на охранение и строительство Великой стены. Из того, что столица династии Мин была перенесена в Пекин, поэтому участок Стены в этом регионе очень крепки, стала самой хорошей частью Великой китайской стены. Длина этого участка стены — 629 км.

八达岭长城

八达岭位于居庸关关沟北口，这里两山夹峙，中通一径，在岭口之间设一关城。长城即从关城的南北两侧依山上筑，长城墙体随山势爬行、工程险峻、气势宏伟。

关城东门提额"居庸外镇"，西门提额"北门锁钥"。

Badaling Great Wall（英文）

Badaling lies at the north end of the Juyongguan Valley, flanked by lofty mountains, and at the entrance to the valley stands a pass. This section of the Great Wall climbs along the mountainsides in a majestic manner.

The plaque on the pass east gate carries inscriptions that read "Outer Town of Juyong," while that on the west gate reads "Strategic Gateway on the Northern Border."

八達嶺長城（日文）

八達嶺は居庸関の入り口となる関溝の北にあたっている。両側は狭い通路をはさむように高い山が立ち並ぶ。この通路に建てられたのは八達嶺長城の関所―居庸関である。城壁は両側の山々の斜面に沿って上に伸びるように構築されている。きわめて険阻なところで、気勢は壮大そのもの。

関所の東門とに西門の上にはそれぞれ「居庸外鎮、「北門鑰匙」と書いた扁額がかかっている。

Badaling（西文）

En el extremo norteño del valle de Guangou, en un camino que pasa entre dos picos, se levantó un castillo que permitiese dominar este punto importante, del cual suben dos murallas por las cuestas de las montañas hacia el norte y el sur. Este es el famoso tramo de la Gran Muralla de Badaling, que integra la parte septentrional del complejo del paso Juyongguan. En sus puertas oriental y occidental se inscriben respectivamente los caracteres de "Fortaleza exterior del paso Juyongguan" y "Cerradura norteña".

Участок Великой стены Бадалин（俄文）

Бадалин находится к северу крепости Цзюйюнгуань. Его крепость была построена в северной части ущелья. На двух сторонах крепости стоят вороты. Над восточными воротами была надпись «Цзюйюнъвайчжэнь» («Внешняя застава Цзюйюнгуаня»), а над западными — «Бэймэньсояо» («Северный замок и ключ»). Одна дорога связывает эти вороты.

바다링장성（韩文）

바다링은 쥐융관 관문의 북쪽에 위치해 있다. 높이 치솟은 두 산사이에 하나의 통로가 있는데 그 사이에 관성을 하나 설치하였다. 장성은 관성의 남북 양쪽에서 시작하여 산세에 따라 구축하였으며 공정이 험준하고 기세가 웅위하다.

동서 관문의 액자에는 각각 "거용외진" 과 "북문쇄열" 이라고 새겨져 있다.

Der Mauerabschnitt Badaling（德文）

Badaling liegt im Norden des Juyongguan-Passes. In der Schlucht Guangou liegt die Guancheng-Festung. An ihrer südlichen und nördlichen Seite sieht man die majestätische Große Mauer.

Die Guancheng-Festung hat ein Ost-und ein Westtor. Am Osttor hängt eine horizontale Tafel mit der Inschrift „Juyong Waizhen" und am Westtor mit der Inschrift „Beimen Suoyao".

La Grande Muraille de Badaling（法文）

Badaling est situé à l'ouverture nord de la vallée de la passe Juyongguan. A cet endroit, deux montagnes encaissent des enceintes fortifiées desservies par un passage au milieu du ravin. La Grande Muraille monte le long des versants des côtés sud et nord du fort. Les portes est et ouest de la passe portent des inscriptions signifiant respectivement "Bourg extérieur de la passe Juyongguan" et "Clé de la porte du nord".

La Grande Muraglia di Badaling（意大利文）

Badaling si trova a nord del Passo di Juyongguan. Un tratto è situato fra i due monti posti l'uno di fronte all'altro. Al centro del valico si erge il passo Guancheng lungo i cui lati meridionale e settentrionale si erge la grande muraglia.

La Porta orientale del passo Guancheng è chiamata "Juyong Waizhen", ovvero Città Esterna del Passo Juyong, mentre quella occidentale è chiamata "Beimen Suoyao", Chiave di accesso alla parte settentrionale di Pechino.

①②③④ 八达岭长城局部
Part of the Badaling Great Wall
八達嶺長城の一部
바다링장성의 국부
Différentes parties de la Grande Muraille de Badaling
Detail des Mauerabschnitts Badaling
Una parte della sezione della Grande Muraglia di Badaling
Часть Великой стены Бадалин
Parte de la Gran Muralla de Badaling

lan
lle
El
zo
ha
im
siempre una "Barrera natural insuperable". Hace algún tiempo fue restaurada.

stratégique, connue pour être une "barrière naturelle". Aujourd'hui, la passe Juyongguan a déjà été restaurée.

이든 '길림(吉林)', '전림(天關)' 이라고도 불린다.
쥐용관장성은 이미 복구되었다.

居庸关长城

　　居庸关距北京50余公里，建于从大同、宣化通往北京的通道中，居庸关所在之处为18公里的关沟中，关沟的南口为入口，北口即八达岭口，地处南北两口之间，关城居于两山夹峙，山形陡峭的峡谷中，有"绝险"、"天险"之称。居庸关长城现已修复。

Juyong Pass（英文）

　　More than 50 kilometers from Beijing, Juyong Pass lies on the passage linking Beijing with Datong and Xuanhua. The pass stands in the middle of an 18-kilometer gorge flanked by steep mountains, at the north end of which is Badaling. The location is described as "unique steepness" and "heaven-sent precipice."

　　The Great Wall section near the Juyong Pass has been restored.

Passo Juyong（意大利文）

　　A 50 chilometri da Pechino, il passo Juyong si trova nei passaggi Beijing – Datong e Beijing-Xuanhua, e dista 18 chilometri da Guangou. La parte meridionale di Guangou costituisce l'accesso del valico, mentre la parte settentrionale è l'accesso di Badaling. Il passo Guancheng, situato nella valle del monte Occidentale è considerato il "più pericoloso" e "il più pericoloso sotto il cielo".

　　La sezione della muraglia di Juyonggua dopo il ristauro.

居庸关城楼
The watchtower on the Juyong Pass
居庸関城楼
쥐융관성루
Tour dressée sur la Grande Muraille au-dessus de la porte de la passe Juyongguan
Wachttürme in Juyongguan
Le torri a Juyongguan
Башня Цзюйюнгуань
Paso Juyongguan

居庸関（日文）

　　居庸関は北京まで50km 離れた、大同と宣化から北京に通じる要路に構築されている。所在の関溝は長さ18kmの峡谷で、峡谷の南口は関溝の入り口にあたり、北口はちょうど八達嶺の入り口になっている。両側の険阻な山々にはさまれて構築された関所－居庸関は「絶険」とか「天険」の称がある。

　　居庸関長城は現在、修復されて一般に開放されている。

Застава Цзюйюнгуань（俄文）

　　Находится примерно в 50 км от Пекина, в проходе Датун провинции Шаньси и Сюаньхуа провинции Хэбэй к Пекину. Была построена в лощине между двумя горами, длиной в 18 км. Цзюйюнгуань является стратегически важным местом.

　　В настоящее время Великая стена заставы Цзюйюнгуань уже была восстановлена.

居庸关长城全景
A view of the Juyong Pass Great Wall
居庸関長城全景
쥐융관장성 전경

居庸关城楼
The watchtower at the Juyong Pass
居庸関城楼
쥐융관성루
Tour dressée sur la Grande Muraille au-dessus de la porte de la passe Juyongguan
Wachttürme in Juyongguan
Le torri a Juyongguan
Башня Цзюйюнгуань
Paso Juyongguan

居庸关长城
The Juyong Pass Great Wall
居庸関長城
쥐융관장성
La Grande Muraille à la passe Juyongguan
Der Mauerabschnitt Juyongguan
La sezione della Grande Muraglia a Juyongguan
Участок Великой стены Цзюйюнгуань
La Gran Muralla en Juyongguan

Juyongguan（西文）

A 50 km. de Beijing se extiende un valle de 18 km. de largo, llamado Guangou, ubicado en el trayecto por el que se llega a la capital desde las ciudades de Datong y Xuanhua. El paso de Juyongguan es el complejo militar que ocupa la zona, desde la entrada en el extremo sureño de la llanura hasta la salida de Badaling, el punto norteño. Debido a su importante posición estratégica, esta parte fue considerada siempre una "Barrera natural insuperable". Hace algún tiempo fue restaurada.

La Passe Juyongguan（法文）

Située à plus de 50 kilomètres au nord-ouest de Beijing, la passe Juyongguan fut construite sur la ligne de communication reliant Datong et Xuanhua à Beijing. Formée de deux cols, la passe Juyongguan se trouve dans une vallée de 18 kilomètres de long. Le col du sud s'appelle Nankou et le col du nord, Badaling. Encaissées entre deux hautes montagnes, les enceintes fortifiées de la passe occupent une position stratégique, connue pour être une "barrière naturelle".

Aujourd'hui, la passe Juyongguan a déjà été restaurée.

쥐융관 （韩文）

쥐융관은 베이징에서 50 여 km 떨어져있다. 다퉁(大同)과 쉬안화(宣化)에서 베이징으로 통하는 요로에서 쥐융관은 길이가 18km 나 되는 골에 위치해 있다. 남쪽 입구는 쥐융관 골의 입구이고 북쪽 입구는 바다링의 관성이며 쥐융관은 남북 입구사이에 위치해 있다. 관성은 우뚝 솟은 두 산봉우리 사이에 위치해 있으며 산세가 험준한 협곡은 "절험(絶險)", "천험(天險)" 이라고 불린다.

쥐융관장성은 이미 복구되었다.

居庸关城楼
The watchtower at the Juyong Pass
居庸関城楼
쥐융관성루
Tour dressée sur la Grande Muraille au-dessus de la porte de la passe
Juyongguan
Wachttürme in Juyongguan
Le torri a Juyongguan
Башня Цзюйюнгуань
Paso Juyongguan

居 庸 关 长 城
The Juyong Pass Great Wall
居 庸 関 長 城
쥐융관장성
La Grande Muraille à la passe Juyongguan
Der Mauerabschnitt Juyongguan
La sezione della Grande Muraglia a Juyongguan
Участок Великой стены Цзюйюнгуань
La Gran Muralla en Juyongguan

居庸关云台

云台原来是一个过街塔建筑。上半部三座塔已毁。云台建于元代，用汉白三砌筑，云台的雕刻有佛像和经咒等。其中最为珍贵的是有六种文字同时刻在一处，即：梵文（古尼泊尔文）、藏文、八思八蒙文、维吾尔文、汉文、西夏文。这是研究古代文学的重要实物。同时也说明了元代中国各族人民文化交流的事实。

La Terrasse des Nuages de la passe Juyongguan （法文）

La Terrasse des Nuages (Yuntai) était à l'origine le soubassement des pagodes enjambant la route. Les trois pagodes reposant sur cette terrasse furent détruites depuis longtemps. La construction de la Terrasse des Nuages date de la dynastie des Yuan. Elle est une maçonnerie de marbre blanc sur laquelle furent sculptées des statues bouddhiques et des mantras. Les plus intéressantes sont les inscriptions gravées en six langues : sanskrit (népalais antique), tibétain, mongol, ouïgoure, han (chinois) et écriture des Xia de l'Ouest (tangout). Ce sont des documents importants pour étudier la littérature ancienne. Par ailleurs, ces inscriptions ont fourni des preuves aux échanges culturels entre les différentes ethnies sous les Yuan.

Plataforma de las Nubes de Juyongguan （西文）

Originalmente perteneció a un conjunto arquitectónico levantado sobre una calle, compuesto por tres pagodas en la parte superior y la base inferior. Construida en la dinastía Yuan, actualmente no queda de ella más que la base, bautizada como Plataforma de las Nubes, que en su superficie está adornada por bajorrelieves de figuras de budas e inscripciones de conjuros. Lo más valioso es que estas letras fueron talladas en seis idiomas: sánscrito (antigua lengua nepalí), tibetano, mongol, uigur, han y xia, lo que las convierte en un documento para el estudio de las lenguas antiguas de China, a la vez que da a conocer la larga historia de intercambio entre las naciones durante la dinastía Yuan.

Cloud Terrace at Juyong Pass （英文）

The Cloud Terrace originally had three towers on the top. First built during the Yuan Dynasty, the marble terrace is decorated with carvings of the Buddha, as well as texts of Buddhist sutras in Sanskrit, Chinese, Tibetan, Mongolian and other two languages. The terrace is significant for research into ancient scripts, and is evidence of cultural exchanges between different ethnic groups during the Yuan Dynasty.

Die Plattform Yuntai des Juyongguan-Passes （德文）

Die Plattform Yuntai war früher das Fendament der drei lamaistischen Pagoden aus der Yuan-Dynastie. Sie ist aus weißem Marmor gebaut. Im Tordurchgang gibt es auf der Wand schöne Reliefs der Buddhafiguren und der kanonischen Schriften des Buddhismus in sechs Sprachen (Sanskrit, Tibetisch, Basima, Uigurisch, Chinesisch und Xixia). Diese buddhistischen Schriften sind für das Studium der Literatur und Religion sowie der Kultur der Yuan-Dynastie von großer Bedeutung.

Башня Юньтай （俄文）

Служила проходом на улицу. Теперь три пагоды на платформе Юньтай уже были разрушены. Эта башня была построена мрамором в 1268 г. На стене ее были вырезаны буддийские изваяния и заклинания. Нужно отметить, что самым дорогим является заклинание на 6 языках: тибетском, китайском, уйгурском, сисяском, санскритском и монгольском. Это важный документ для изучения древней литературы. И сильно доказывает, что в династии Юань развивались культурные обмены между народами разных национальностей.

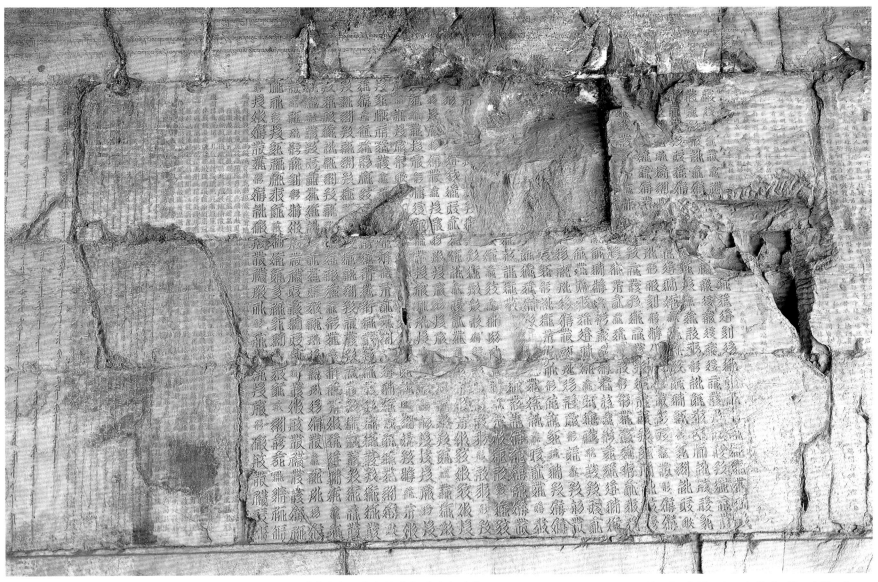

云台内的六种文字石刻
Stone inscriptions in six languages at the Cloud Terrace
雲台の六種文字石刻

원타이의 6 가지 문자가 새겨진 비석
Inscriptions gravées en six langues sur le mur de la Terrasse des Nuages

Sechsrprachige Inschriften innerhalb der Yuntai-Plattform
Rilievo di iscrizioni in sei lingue nell'interno di Yuntai
Заклинание на 6 языках на стене платформы Юньтай
Letras inscritas en la Plataforma de las Nubes, en Juyongguan

Yuntai a Juyonggua（意大利文）

In origine Yuntai si trovava al centro della strada: un edificio di marmo bianco costruito all'epoca della dinastia Yuan, sul quale le tre pagode in cima sono oggi in stato di abbandono. Yuntai presenta dei rilievi di Buddha e testi sacri buddisti incisi in sei lingue: sanskrito, tibetano, mongolo Basiba, uiguro, cinese e xixia. Questi testi sono un importante elemento per lo studio della letteratura antica e costituiscono la testimonianza degli scambi culturali fra diversi gruppi etnici nel paese.

쥐융관 원타이(雲台)（韩文）

원타이는 본래 길을 가로 질러 지은 탑이다. 위의 3 개 탑은 이미 파괴된지 오래다. 원타이는 원나라 시기에 한백옥으로 구축하였다. 원타이의 조각에는 불상과 경문 등이 있다. 진귀한 것은 6 가지 문자가 동시에 조각어 있다는 것이다. 즉, 범어(고대네팔문), 티베트어, 몽골어, 위구르어, 한어, 서하(오르도스)문이다. 이것은 고대문학을 연구하는 중요한 실물인 동시 원나라 시기에 중국의 여러 소수민족 사이에 문화교류가 발생하였다는 것을 설명한다.

居庸関の雲台（日文）

雲台は、もともとは街をまたぐ橋式塔―過街塔であった。上にある 3 つの塔は早くも壊されてしまった。元代に漢白玉石を畳んでつくったもの。さまざまな仏像や経咒が彫られたが、梵語（古代ネパール語）、チベット語、八思八モンゴル語、ウイグル語、漢語と西夏語の彫刻はもっとも珍しい。これらの文字は中国の古代文学を研究するための大切な物証であり、元代中国の各民族の文化交流を実証している。

慕田峪长城

慕田峪长城位于北京东北郊怀柔境内，西接居庸关长城，东连古北口长城，离昌平境内的明陵区仅 30 公里。慕田峪地处偏僻山区，自然环境保护良好，植被覆盖率达 70%以上。

Mutianyu Great Wall（英文）

Situated at Huairou District in the northeastern suburbs of Beijing, 30 kilometers from the Ming Tombs in Changping District, the Mutianyu Great Wall connects the Juyong Pass in the west, with Gubeikou in the east. This area is mountainous and densely forested.

慕田峪長城（日文）

慕田峪長城は北京市東北郊外の懷柔県内にある。西は居庸関に接し、東は古北口に通じ、昌平県内の明の十三陵まではわずか30ｋｍしか離れていない。山の奥深くにあるため、自然環境はよく保たれており、植生の被覆率は70％以上に達している。

무톈위장성（韓文）

무톈위장성은 베이징 동북교외 화이러우 경내에 있으며 서쪽은 쥐융관과 이어지고 동쪽은 구베이커우(古北口)와 이어졌으며 창핑의 명능과 30km 떨어졌다. 무톈위는 편벽한 산구에 위치해 있으며 자연 환경이 잘 보호되고 식물피복율이 70% 이상에 달한다.

La Grande Muraille de Mutianyu（法文）

Située dans l'arrondissement de Huairou aux environs nord-est de Beijing, la Grande Muraille de Mutianyu est adjacente à la passe Juyongguan à l'ouest et à la passe de Gubeikou à l'est. Seulement 30 kilomètres la séparent de la nécropole des Ming. En raison de sa position dans les montagnes reculées, l'environnement naturel est bien préservé à Mutianyu et le taux de couverture forestière y est supérieur à 70%.

Der Mauerabschnitt Mutianyu（德文）

Der Mauerabschnitt Mutianyu liegt innerhalb des Stadtbezirkes Huairou im nordöstlichen Vorort Beijings, 30 km von den Ming-Gräbern entfernt. Er grenzt im Westen an den Juyongguan-Pass und im Osten an den Mauerabschnitt Gubeikou. Das örtliche Ökosystem ist gut erhalten. Die Vegetationsfläche beträgt über 70 Prozent.

La Gran Muralla de Mutianyu（西文）

Mutianyu se encuentra en el distrito de Huairou, en el suburbio noreste de Beijing, unido por el Oeste con el paso Juyongguan y por el Este con la sección de Gubeikou y dista 30 km. de las Trece Tumbas de Ming, en el distrito de Changping. Por su ubicación en la zona montañosa, este tramo de la Gran Muralla se destaca por el hermoso paisaje natural y una cobertura forestal de más del 70%.

La sezione della Grande Muraglia di Mutianyu（意大利文）

La sezione della Grande Muraglia di Mutianyu si trova nel territorio del distretto di Huairou, nella periferia nord-orientale di Pechino, collegato con Juyonggua a ovest e Gubeikou a est, a 30 chilometri dall'area delle tombe Ming nel territorio del distretto di Changping. Mutianyu è situata in una remota area montuosa per cui qui l'ambiente non è inquinato ed il 70% della sua superficie è coperta da una ricca vegetazione.

Участок Великой Китайской стены Мутяньюй（俄文）

Находится в 20 км от северо-запада района Хуайжоу Пекина, в 30 км от могилам минских императоров. Здесь растительность густа, более 70% земли покрыты травой, лесом и фруктовыми деревьями.

慕田峪长城局部
Sections of the Mutianyu Great Wall
慕田峪長城の一部
무텐위장성의 국부
Différentes parties de la Grande Muraille de Mutianyu
Detail des Mauerabschnitts Mutianyu
La sezione parziale della Grande Muraglia di Mutianyu
Часть Великой стены Мутяньюй
Parte de la Gran Muralla de Mutianyu

慕田峪正关台

正关台位于山谷要冲，关台上三座敌楼相连并立，中间一座为空心敌楼，两侧为实心。这种建筑形式，北京地区仅此一处。

Mutianyu Pass （英文）

Guarding the entrance to a valley, this pass has three interlinked watchtowers. This structure is unique to the Great Wall.

慕田峪の正関台 （日文）

山谷の要衝の地にある。関台の上にある 3 つの望楼は相連なるように建てられており、真ん中の 1 つは中空のもので、両側のは中が詰まっている。このような望楼は、北京地域ではこれしかない。

무톈위정관타이 （韩文）

산골짜기의 요충지에 있으며 관대 위에는 3 개의 망루를 병열하여 구축하였는데 가운데의 것은 속이 빈 망루이며 양쪽은 속이 찬 망루이다. 이런 건축형식은 베이징지역에서 하나밖에 없다.

La terrasse principale de la passe de Mutianyu （法文）

Sur la terrasse de la passe qui occupe le point stratégique de la vallée se dressent trois tours de guet rangée sur une ligne, dont celle au centre est une tour creuse, tandis que celles des deux côtés, pleines. Cette forme architecturale est unique dans la région de Beijing.

Der Zhenguantai-Pass in Mutianyu （德文）

Dieser Pass befindet sich in einem Bergtal und besteht aus drei nebeneinander liegenden Wachttürmen und einem Südtor, was eine Seltenheit gegenüber anderen Pässen auf der ganzen Strecke der Großen Mauer ist.

Plataforma Zhengguantai de Mutianyu （西文）

Localizada en un punto de gran importancia estratégica dentro del valle. Cuenta con tres atalayas, la del medio de las cuales es hueca, mientras las de los laterales macizas, única arquitectura de su tipo en toda la región de Beijing.

Zhengguantai a Mutianyu （意大利文）

Tre torrette di guardia costuituiscono Zhengguantai, cava al centro mentre le altre due sono compatte, una struttura unica nel suo genere nell'area di Pechino.

Чжэньгуаньтай （俄文）

Находится во входе в Мутяньюй, состоит из трех башен с террасой. Центральная башня пустотела, а другие две из цельных кирпичей. Такое сооружение не знает себе равных в Пекине.

慕田峪 "箭扣" 长城

　　山峰上两岩分离，有如鹰嘴朝天，下临数十丈深渊，为控制这座高峰，在两岩之间搭上铁梁，使长城凌空飞架而过，其险峻令人惊叹。

Jiankou Great Wall at Mutianyu （英文）

Two rocks on the mountaintop look like an eagle's beak, beneath which is a deep gulf. The Great Wall spans the two rocks.

慕田峪の「箭扣」長城 （日文）

頭を挙げて空を見る鷹の、開いた嘴のような切り立った岩壁の間に鉄桁をかけてつくった城壁。

무톈위 "젠커우" 장성 （韓文）

산봉우리에 있는 두 암석은 분리되어 마치 독수리의 부리가 하늘을 향하는 것 같으며 밑에는 깊은 골짜기가 있다. 산봉우리의 두 암석사이에 철근을 가로놓고 장성이 허공에서 건느게 하였는데 그 험준함은 사람들로 하여금 경탄을 금치 못하게 한다.

La Grande Muraille Jiankou à Mutianyu （法文）

Les deux pics de la montagne dressés comme le bec d'aigle pointant vers le ciel surplombent une vallée de plusieurs dizaines de mètres de profondeur. La Grande Muraille repose sur les poutres soutenues par ces deux pics. Cette situation périlleuse est vraiment impressionnante.

Die „Jiankou-Strecke" des Mauerabschnitts Mutianyu （德文）

Diese Mauerstrecke wurde auf einem Stahlbalken zwischen zwei steilen Felsen auf einem Berggipfel gebaut und sieht von weitem gesehen wie ein „fliegender Adler" aus.

La Gran Muralla Jiankou de Mutianyu （西文）

Para dominar la altura de dos picos empinados, estos fueron atravesados con dos barras de hierro, sobre las cuales se levantaron los muros de la Gan Muralla por encima de las cumbres.

Стена «Цзянькоу» (зарубка стрелы) （俄文）

Как название показывает данный участок Великой Китайской стены вроде бы вешает над краем скалы

La muraglia "Jiankou" a Mutianyu （意大利文）

Le due rocce separate il cima al monte sembrano il becco di un'aquila rivolta verso il cielo. In basso, sotto le rocce c'è un dirupo di dieci metri di profondità. Qui la grande Muraglia fu costruita su travi di ferro poggiate sulle rocce.

慕田峪箭扣长城雪景
The Mutianyu Jiankou Great Wall in snow
慕田峪箭扣長城の雪景色
무톈위젠커우장성의 설경
La Grande Muraille Jiankou à Mutianyu couverte de neige
Winterlandschaft in Mutianyu
La muraglia Jiankou a Mutianyu sotto la neve
Стена «Цзянькоу» в Мутяньюй под снегом
Paisaje después de la nieve en la Gran Muralla de Jiankou en Mutianyu

慕田峪箭扣长城
The Jiankou Great Wall at Mutianyu
慕田峪の箭扣長城
무톈위젠커우장성
La Grande Muraille Jiankou à Mutianyu
Die Jiankou-Strecke des Mauerabschnitts Mutianyu
La muraglia Jiankou a Mutianyu
Стена «Цзянькоу» в Мутяньюй
La Gran Muralla de Jiankou en Mutianyu

司马台长城

　　司马台长城位于北京密云区，与金山岭长城相连。这里地势险要、视野开阔、气势磅礴。这段长城极有特色，几乎每个深沟峡谷和险要山头都有一座敌楼，短短25公里之间就设有敌楼站台140多座。而其中的望京楼、仙女楼、大、小金山楼等更是美不胜收。这里还有仅容一人攀登、刀削般颠峰上的单边石砌城墙，真所谓一夫当关，万夫莫开。

Simatai Great Wall（英文）

The Simatai Great Wall in Miyun District is connected to the Jinshanling Great Wall. It boasts a precipitous location and wide vistas. Along this section of the Great Wall, almost every gorge or mountaintop has a watchtower. -- more than 140 watchtowers are located within a distance of 25 kilometers, of which the most spectacular are the Capital-Watching Tower, Fairy Tower and Greater and Lesser Jinshan Towers.

司馬台長城（日文）

　　北京市密雲県内にある。金山嶺長城とは相連なっている。周辺は地形が険阻そのもので、視野は広い。ほとんどすべての溝や谷と山に1つの望楼があることは、この区間の長城の特徴である。総延長は25kmしかないが、140あまりもの望楼がある。望京楼、仙女楼、大・小金山楼などの望楼はもっとも美しい。ほかに狭くて体を斜めにしないと通り過ぎれない長城、切り立った岩壁の上につくった片側城壁の長城など、いろいろな険を極める城壁がある。

司马台望京楼长城
The Capital-Watching Tower on the Simatai Great Wall
司馬台長城の望京楼区間
쓰마타이왕징러우장성
La Grande Muraille de Simatai près de la Tour "Ayant vue sur Beijing"
Die Wangjinglou-Strecke des Mauerabschnitts Simatai
La Torrettta d'Osservazione su Pechino della Muraglia di Simatai
Дозорная башня Ванцзиньлоу в Сыматае
La Torre de la Mira de Beijing, en la Gran Muralla de Simatai

① 司马台鸳鸯湖
Yuanyang Lake at Simatai
司馬台の鴛鴦湖
쓰마타이위안양호
Le lac des Canards mandarins à Simatai
Der Yuanyang-See in Simatai
Il lago Yuanyang a Simatai
Озеро Юаньянху в Сыматай
Lago Yuanyang en Simatai

La sezione della muraglia di Simatai（意大利文）

Situata nel distretto di Miyun a Pechino, la sezione della muraglia di Simatai è collegata alla sezione della muraglia di Jinshanling. Qui la posizione geografica scoscesa e strategicamente importante presenta una visuale aperta. Questa sezione ha un carattere particolare: quasi in ogni valle, gola e cima è presente una torretta di guardia. Lunga 25 chilometri, questa sezione conta 140 torrette di guardia. Le torrette d'Osservazione su Pechino, della Fata, Xiaojin e Dajin sono maestose e offrono una magnifica visuale. La torretta Danbian (unilaterale) si affaccia su un dirupo praticamente inaccessibile.

La Grande Muraille de Simatai（法文）

Située dans l'arrondissement de Miyun à Beijing, la Grande Muraille de Simatai est liée à la Grande Muraille de Jinshanling. A cet endroit, les falaises à pic offrent un spectacle grandiose. Presque chaque ravin profond et chaque sommet important sont munis d'une tour de guet. Sur un tronçon de muraille long de 25 kilomètres, on compte plus de 140 tours de guet et terrasses dont les plus belles sont la Tour "Ayant vue sur Beijing" (Wangjinglou), la Tour de la Fée (Xiannülou), et la grande et la petite Tours Jinshan (montagne d'or). A cet endroit, on trouve des murs simples en pierre construits sur les falaises aux parois verticales, présentant une topographie si difficile d'accès que l'on la qualifie par le terme "Un homme prend la clé, dix mille hommes n'ouvrent pas".

Участок Великой Китайской стены Сыматай（俄文）

Находится в районе Миюнь Пекина, связывается с участком Великой стены Цзиньшаньлин. Данный участок стены располагает своей особенностью. Почти в каждом ущелье и обрывистом месте горы были построены дозорные башни. На расстоянии 50 хуали (1 хуали = 500 м.) есть более 140 дозорных башен. Среди них башни Ванцзинлоу, Сяньнюйлоу, Цзиньшаньлоу очень известны. Здесь еще есть односторонняя стена, которая была построена на гребне горы.

②③④ 司马台长城局部
Part of the Simatai Great Wall
司馬台長城の一部
쓰마타이장성의 국부
Différentes parties de la Grande Muraille de Simatai
Detail des Mauerabschnitts Simatai
La sezione parziale della Muraglia di Simatai
Участок Великой Китайской стены Сыматай
Parte de la Gran Muralla de Simatai

Der Mauerabschnitt Simatai（德文）

Dieser Mauerabschnitt liegt innerhalb des Stadtbezirkes Miyun und ist mit dem Mauerabschnitt Jinshanling verbunden. Er ist 25 km lang und hat insgesamt über 140 Wachttürme, von denen der Wangjing-, der Xiannü-, der Dajinshan- und der Xiaojinshan-Wachtturm am bekanntesten sind. Die Simatai-Mauer schlängelt sich durch Bergrücken und ist besonders schwer passierbar.

쓰마타이장성（韩文）

베이징 미윈에 위치해 있는 쓰마타이 장성은 진산링장성과 이어져 있다. 이곳은 지세가 험준하고 웅위하며 시야가 넓게 트인다. 이 구간의 장성은 아주 특점이다. 거의 모든 깊은 골짜기, 협곡, 험요한 산봉우리마다 망루가 하나씩 구축되어 있는데 50 화리(1 화리 =500 미터) 사이에 망루가 무려 140 여개나 있다. 그 중 왕징루(望京樓), 셴뉘루(仙女樓), 다진산루(大金山樓), 샤오진산루(小金山樓) 등은 아름답기 그지없다. 칼로 깍아놓은 듯한 산꼭대기에 돌로 쌓은 단벤성벽(얇은 성벽으로 한쪽은 사람이 통과할 수 없는 험준한 지세이다.)이 있는데 빈 몸으로만 올라갈 수 있어 그야말로 한 병사가 지키고 있으면 천군 만마로도 공략할 수 없는 요새이다.

La Gran Muralla de Simatai（西文）

Situado en el distrito de Miyun, este tramo de la Gran Muralla está conectado con la sección de Jinshanling. Es muy afamado por su importante ubicación, vista abierta y aire majestuoso. Además, se caracteriza por las atalayas que ocupan los valles y picos a lo largo de 25 km., cuyo número supera las 140. Entre estas se distinguen las de la Mira de Beijing, Adas y la Mayor y Menor de la Colina Dorada. Parte del trayecto de la fortificación de la zona se yergue al borde de un peligroso precipicio, desde el que aprecia una vista imponente.

古北口长城

古北口与居庸关东西对峙，西北为居庸关，东北为古北口，是北京两个重要门户。这里的长城修筑得十分牢固。

Gubeikou Great Wall （英文）

Gubeikou faces the Juyong Pass in the northwest. These were strategically two most important passes in the Beijing area.

古北口長城 （日文）

居庸関とは相対峙するようにある。居庸関は西北のほうにあり、東北にあるのは古北口である。二つとも北京の大切な門戸である。きわめて堅固なように構築されている。

구베이커우 장성 （韩文）

구베이커우와 쥐융관은 동서로 마주향해 있으며 서북쪽은 쥐융관이고 동북쪽은 구베이커우이며 베이징의 두 개의 중요한 관문이다. 이곳의 장성은 아주 든든하게 수건되었다.

La Grande Muraille de Gubeikou （法文）

La passe de Gubeikou et la passe Juyongguan qui se font face respectivement au nord-est et au nord-ouest sont deux importantes entrées de Beijing. La Grande Muraille de Gubeikou est très solide.

Der Mauerabschnitt Gubeikou （德文）

Dieser Mauerabschnitt liegt zwischen den Bergen Panlong und Wohu im Norden des Stadtbezirkes Miyun und ist sehr solide gebaut. Gubeikou gehörte mit dem Juyongguan-Pass zu den zwei wichtigen Toren Beijings.

La sezione della Grande Muraglia di Gubeikou （意大利文）

Gubeikou e Juyongguan sorgono una di fronte all'altro in direzione est-ovest. La parte nord-occidente è Juyongguam, mentre a nord-est si trova Gubeikou, entrambe importanti per la protezione di Pechino. La sezione della Grande Muraglia a Gubeikou è forte e solida.

Участок Великой Китайской стены Губэйкоу （俄文）

Находится на севере уезда Миюнь Пекина. Губэйкоу с заставой Цзюйюнгуань являются важным воротами к Пекину. Поэтому здешняя стена очень крепка.

La Gran Muralla de Gubeikou （西文）

Igual al paso Juyongguan, la sección Gubeikou desempeña un rol importante en la defensa del norte de Beijing, de ahí que sus muros sean muy reforzados.

沿河城敌台

沿河城位于门头沟区西北部的崇山峻岭中，在太行山余脉黄草梁、清水尖两山夹峙之中。这里地势险要，永定河奔腾回旋，为军事重镇。

Yanhecheng Watchtower（英文）

Hidden amidst lofty mountains in northwestern Mentougou District, Yanhecheng is flanked by Huangcaoliang and Qingshuijian, both extensions of the Taihang Mountains. Occupying a precipitous location, it was a town of military importance. The Yongding River runs through the area.

沿河城望楼（日文）

門頭溝西北部を走る太行山の余脈・黄草梁と清水尖の奥深くにある。地勢が険を極め、永定河が山々を取り巻いて流れる軍事重鎮である。

옌허(沿河)성 망루（韩文）

옌허성은 먼터우거우구 서북부의 뭇산 속에 위치해 있다. 타이항산맥의 지맥인 황차오량(黄草梁)과 칭수이젠(清水尖) 두 산사이의 골짜기에 있다. 이곳은 지세가 힘준하고 융딩허가 굽이쳐 흐르고 있으며 아주 중요한 군사 요충지이다.

La tour de guet de Yanhecheng（法文）

Située dans les hautes montagnes dans le nord-ouest de l'arrondissement de Mentougou, Yanhecheng est resserrée entre le mont Huangcaoliang et le pic Qingshuijian, appartenant à un chaînon des monts Taihang. Dotée d'une topographie accidentée et difficile d'accès et entourée par la rivière Yongding, Yanhecheng était une ville de garnison d'importance stratégique.

Wachtturm der Festung Yanhecheng（德文）

Yanhecheng ist eine bekannte Festung aus der Ming-Dynastie. Sie befindet sich im Yingdinghe-Flusstal zwischen den Bergen Huangcaoling und Qingshuijian im Nordwesten des Stadtbezirkes Fangshan.

La Torretta di Yanhecheng（意大利文）

Yanhecheng si trova fra la catena montuosa di Taihang e il monte Qingshuijian nella parte nord-occidentale della regione di Mentougou. Grazie alla sua posizione geografica scoscesa e al fiume Yongding che scorre qui, Yanhecheng era una cittadina strategicamente importante dal punto di vista militare.

Дозорная башня Яньхэчэн（俄文）

Городок Яньхэчэн находится в горах северо-запада района Мэньтоугоу. Здесь местность неприступна. Поэтому городок является стратегически важным городком.

Atalayas en Yanhecheng（西文）

Yanhecheng, trascendental punto estratégico, se encuentra entre las montañas del noroeste del distrito de Mentougou, en Beijing, entre dos picos y a la orilla del río Yongdinghe.

黄花城长城

黄花城长城位于怀柔区西北，昌平明陵东北，为京师北门重要关隘。

Huanghuacheng Great Wall（英文）

Located northeast of the Ming Tombs in Changping District, the Huanghuacheng Great Wall in northwestern Huairou District is regarded as the north gate of Beijing.

黄花城（日文）

懐柔区西北、昌平区の明の十三陵の東北にある。北京の北を護る大切な長城である。

황화성 장성（韩文）

화이러우구의 서북쪽에 있는 창핑 명능 동북쪽에 위치해 있으며 베이징 북문의 중요한 요충지이다.

Huanghuacheng（法文）

Située dans le nord-ouest de l'arrondissement de Huairou et au nord-est de la nécropole des Ming, Huanghuacheng était une importante passe au nord de Beijing.

Huanghuacheng（德文）

Huanghuacheng liegt im Nordwesten des Stadtbezirkes Huairou und im Nordosten der Ming-Gräber und ist eine wichtige Festung im Norden Beijings.

Huanghuacheng（意大利文）

Situata a nord-ovest della zona di Huairou, e a nord-est rispetto all'area delle tombe Ming a Changping, Huanghuacheng era un passo importante per l'accesso settentrionale a Pechino

Хуанхуачэн（俄文）

Находится на северо-западе района Хуайжоу, на северо-востоке от могил минских императоров. Является важным северным проходом в столицу-Пекин.

Huanghuacheng（西文）

Huanghuacheng, paso clave del norte de Beijing. Se sitúa al noroeste del distrito de Changping y al noreste de las Trece Tumbas de Ming, en el distrito de Changping.

金山岭长城

　　金山岭长城位于北京市密云县与河北滦平县交界地带，因修建在大小金山上而得名。北段长城是万里长城最具代表性的工程之一。

　　金山岭长城最大特点是敌楼密集，一般在100米左右建敌楼一座，有的随地形之变仅相距50米。敌楼根据箭窗多少有"三眼楼"、"四眼楼"、"五眼楼"之分。而且楼顶的建筑形式也多姿多样。

　　金山岭长城地处险要，山势起伏不断，工程建造精湛，常有云海涌动于敌楼之间，加上北国苍茫飞雪，是长城绝佳的赏景之地

Jinshanling Great Wall （英文）

The Jinshanling Great Wall lies on the border between Beijing's Miyun County and Hebei's Luanping County, and its name comes from the Larger and Lesser Jinshan Mountains, on which the wall were constructed. Its northern part is regarded as one of the most spectacular sections of the Great Wall.

This section of the Great Wall has numerous watchtowers that are distributed at an average interval of 100 meters. The nearest two watchtowers are as close as 50 meters. Some watchtowers have three loopholes, some four and some five. Also, they vary in architectural style.

The superbly designed Great Wall at Jinshanling snakes along rolling mountains, and the nearby valley is often shrouded in haze. It is an ideal destination for tourists, especially in winter when it is covered in white snow.

金山嶺長城 （日文）

北京市密雲県と河北省灤平県とが境を接するところにある。大・小金山の上に構築されていることから名づけられた。この長城の北区間は、万里の長城においてももっと代表的なものである。

望楼が多いことは金山嶺長城の最大な特徴である。一般的には100mおきに一つの望楼があるが、ところによっては50mしかない区間にも望楼が構築されている。望楼は「箭窓」（矢の射撃孔）の多少によって、「四眼楼」と「五眼楼」とに分かれ、屋根の形もまちまちである。

城壁はきわめて険阻な山々に美しく構築され、周辺は時々に霧や雲が立ち込める。雪のときは、長城の雪景色を楽しむ最適な場所である。

진산링장성 （韩文）

진산링장성은 베이징시 미원현과 허베이 롼핑(灤平)현의 인접지에 있으며 다진산과 샤오진산 위에 수건되어 붙인 이름이다. 북쪽 장성 중 가장 대표성을 가지고 있는 공정 중의 하나이다.

진산링장성의 가장 큰 특점은 망루가 밀집된 것인데 보통 100m 정도에 하나씩 구축되어 있는데 지형에 따라 50m 를 사이두고 구축된 곳도 있다. 망루는 활을 쏠 수 있는 구멍 개수에 따라 "싼옌루(三眼樓)", "쓰옌루(四眼樓)", "우옌루(五眼樓)" 로 구분된다. 뿐 만 아니라 누각 지붕의 건축형식도 아주 여러 가지이다.

진산링장성 부근은 지세가 험준하구 산세 기복이 크며 장성도 아주 조예가 깊게 구축되었다. 산골짜기는 운애가 명멸한데다 겨울에는 눈꽃이 만발하여 장성을 관상하기 아주 좋은 곳이다.

①②③④ 金山岭长城局部
Part of the Jinshanling Great Wall
金山嶺長城の一部
진신링장성의 국부
Différentes parties de la Grande Muraille de Jinshanling
Detail des Mauerabschnitts Jinshanling
La sezione parziale della Muraglia di Jinshanling
Участок Великой Китайской стены Цзиньшаньлин
Parte de la Gran Muralla de Jinshanling

⑤ 金山岭长城大金山楼
The Larger Jinshan Tower on the Jinshanling Great Wall
金山嶺長城の大金山楼
진산링장성의 다진산루
La Tour du grand mont Jinshan sur la Grande Muraille de Jinshanling
Der Große Jinshan-Wachtturm in Jinshanling
La Torretta Dajinshan della Muraglia a Jinshanling
Башня Дацзиньшаньлоу в Цзиньшаньлин
Torre Dajinshan en Jinshanling

La sezione della Grande Muraglia di Jinshanling （意大利文）

La sezione della Grande Muraglia di Jinshanling si trova lungo il confine tra il distretto di Miyun di Pechino e il distretto di Ruanping, nella provincia dello Hebei. Il suo nome deriva dalla sua posizione fra i monti Dajinshan e Xiaojinshan. È un'opera rappresentativa della Grande Muraglia.

Lungo la Grande Muraglia di Jinshanling sono presenti numerose torrette di guardia in diversi stili a distanze variabili fra i 50 e i 100 metri l'una dall'altra. Secondo il numero di fori da tirro, le torri si dividono in: torre con tre fori da tirro, con quattro fori e con cinque fori. Le torri sono di fogge svariate: quadrate, piatte e alcune dotate di fori.

La Grande Muraglia di Jinshanling costituisce una struttura ondulata che segue la forma naturale delle montagne, spesso avvolte dalle nuvole. La sua posizione geografica la rende un luogo incantevole in cui ammirare il paesaggio e percepire la maestosità della Grande Muraglia.

La Grande Muraille de Jinshanling （法文）

La Grande Muraille de Jinshanling est située à la limite de l'arrondissement de Miyun de la municipalité de Beijing et du district de Luanping de la province du Hebei. La muraille repose sur le grand et le petit monts Jinshan, d'où son nom. La Grande Muraille de Jinshanling est un des tronçons les plus représentatifs de l'ensemble.

La plus grande caractéristique de la Grande Muraille de Jinshanling consiste dans la densité des tours de guet. L'espace entre les deux tours de guet voisines y est normalement d'une centaine de mètres. Mais selon la topographie, les deux tours ne sont parfois distantes que de 50 mètres. D'après le nombre des meurtrières, on y distingue les tours à trois, quatre ou cinq meurtrières. Les formes architecturales des toits des tours sont également fort variées.

A Jinshanling, la topographie est fort accidentée, les montagnes ondulent et les nuages voilent souvent les monts et les vaux. En hiver, la neige tombe à gros flocons. Tout cela fait de la Grande Muraille de Jinshanling le lieu optimal pour admirer les beaux paysages.

Цзиньшаньлин （俄文）

Участок Великой Китайской стены Цзиньшаньлин находится в 120 км от Пекина, на границе уезда Миюнь и уезда Луаньпин. Северный участок его является одним из самых типичных участков Великой стены.

Самой большой особенностью Цзиньшаньлин является массирование дозорных башен. Они были построены с интервалами в 50-200 метров. По численности амбразур башни разделяются на трехглазые, четырехглазые и пятиглазые башни.

Облачное море, часто появляющееся среди гор и снег делают Цзиньшаньлин красивым.

Der Mauerabschnitt Jinshanling （德文）

Dieser Mauerabschnitt liegt auf dem Großen und dem Kleinen Jinshan-Berg zwischen dem Bezirk Miyun der Stadt Beijing und dem Kreis Luanping der Provinz Hebei. Er ist der prächtigste Abschnitt der weltbekannten Großen Muaer aus der Ming-Zeit.

Die Jinshanling-Mauer zeichnet sich durch ihre dicht nebenander liegenden Wachttürme aus. Im Abstand von 50 bis 100 Metern gibt es einen Wachtturm. Jeder Wachtturm hat drei, vier oder fünf Schießscharten. Ihre Decken sind flach, gewölbt oder segel- und kassettenförmig.

Die Landschaft in Jinshanling ist das ganze Jahr hindurch faszinierend. Im Sommer und Herbst sieht man hier oft Wolkenmeer und im Winter sieht Jinshanling wie eine Schneewelt aus, auf der sich die Große Mauer wie eine Schlange schlängelt.

La Gran Muralla de Jinshanling （西文）

Jinshanling se sitúa en el límite del distrito de Miyun, de Beijing, y el distrito de Luanping, de la provincia de Hebei, cuyo nombre Jinshan (en chino significa "colina dorada") provienen de dos montañas homónimas. Es la parte más representativa en el recorrido norteño de la Gran Muralla.

Se caracteriza por tener atalayas muy cercanas y unidas, por lo general a una distancia de 100 m. una de otra, que en algunos tramos se reduce a sólo 50 m. Según el número de aberturas para tirar flechas, las atalayas fueron bautizadas como Torre de tres, cuatro o cinco agujeros, y sus modelos de construcción son muy variados.

Durante el mar de nubes que se forman en los valles o después de la nieve son los mejores momentos para contemplar la belleza de la Gran Muralla, de extraordinaria calidad constructiva, que atraviesa las empinadas cordilleras.

单边长城

　　单边长城仅是一堵薄墙，常砌筑在山势险，山脊高耸且薄，边墙外难以人马通过的地段。这是限于地形迫不得已采用的建筑类型。

Single-Sided Great Wall（英文）

The Great Wall was often constructed with only one side on steep and lofty cliffs, for ease of access.

片側城壁の長城（日文）

片側城壁とは名のとおり、片側しかレンガを畳まなかった城壁のことで、多くは険阻な高い山の急勾配に築かれた。一般の城壁の築造ができない場合に考え出されたものである。

단볜성벽장성（韓文）

단볜성벽이 기타 성벽과의 구별은 하나의 얇은 벽이라는 것이다. 흔히 산세가 험준하고 산등성이가 좁은 곳에 구축하였는데 성벽밖은 사람이나 말이 통과하기 어렵다. 지형 때문에 부득불 사용하는 건축유형이다.

La Grande Muraille à murs simples（法文）

La Grande Muraille à murs simples n'est qu'une muraille mince, construite souvent sur les cimes abruptes difficiles d'accès. C'est la topographie de l'endroit qui impose cette forme architecturale.

Danbianqiang（德文）

Bei Danbianqiang handelt es sich die auf dem Bergrücken gebaute einseitige Steinmauer, die besonders schwer passierbar ist.

Muri *Danbian* (unilaterali)（意大利文）

I muri *Danbian* si ergono su un dirupo molto ripido in una posizione geografica scoscesa e strategicamente importante molto difficile da attraversare a cavallo.

Односторонняя стена（俄文）

Она отличается тонкостью и тем, что данная стена была построена на узком и высоком гребне горы. За данной стеной человеку и коню трудно проходить. Из-за ландшафта пришлось выбрать такую архитектурную форму.

Muralla de un solo muro （西文）

　　Por lo general la muralla tiene un muro exterior y otro interior, pero en una de sus secciones sólo fue posible levantar uno de ellos por lo angosta que resultaba para erigir las dos partes la cresta de la montaña, que no dejaba espacio para el paso de las personas o los caballos. Es una medida adoptada según la condición local.

长城城墙上的石道
A stone-paved slope on the Great Wall
城壁の上の石畳道
장성성벽위의 석도（石道）
Une allée pavée sur la Grande Muraille
Steinweg auf der Großen Mauer
Il sentiere di pietra sul muro della Grande Muraglia
Каменная дорога на стене
Camino en el muro de la Gran Muralla

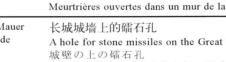

长城的障墙
A defense wall on the Great Wall
城壁の上の障壁
장성위의 담장
Un mur de barrière sur la Grande Muraille

Sperrmauer der Großen Mauer
Ostacoli sul muro della Grande Muraglia
Стена-преграда
Muro de la Gran Muralla

长城城墙上的射孔
Loopholes on the Great Wall
城壁の上の射撃孔
장성성벽위의 총안(銃眼)
Meurtrières ouvertes dans un mur de la

Grande Muraille
Schießscharten der Großen Mauer
Due fori da tiro sul muro della Grande Muraglia
Амбразуры для стрельбы из лука
Agujero para arquero de la Gran Muralla

长城城墙上的关门
A gateway on the Great Wall
城壁の上の関門
장성성벽위의 관문
Porte percée dans un mur de la Grande Muraille

Das Guanmen-Tor der Großen Mauer
Un ingresso sul muro della Grande
Muraglia
Ворота на стене
Puerta en el muro de la Gran Muralla

长城城墙上的礌石孔
A hole for stone missiles on the Great Wall
城壁の上の礌石孔
장성성벽위의 돌을 떨어뜨리는 구멍
Trou pour le lancement des blocs de pierre

faits dans un mur de la Grande Muraille
Das Leishi-Loch der Großen Mauer
Un foro per lanciare pietre sul muro della
Grande Muraglia
Дыры для камня на стене
Agujero para lanzar la piedra en la Gran Muralla

万里长城唯一的一幅影壁浮雕
The only screen with relief carving along the Great Wall
万 里 長 城 唯 一 の 目 隠 壁 の 浮 雕
만리장성에서　유일한　영벽부조
Mur-écran aux sculptures, unique en son genre sur la Grande Muraille
Der einzige Wandschirm der Großen Mauer
L'unico rilievo sul muro della Grande Muraglia
Единственная стена с барельефами Великой Китайской стены
Bajorrelieve Yingbi, el único en la Gran Muralla

黄崖关长城

　　黄崖关长城位于天津市蓟县迤北30千米处，距天津市100多千米。黄崖关长城始建于北齐天保七年（556），明代隆庆（1567-1572）年间，又包砖大修。全段长城建在陡峭的山脊上。这里墙台敌楼，边城掩体，水关烟墩，古寨营盘等各项设施完备，关外数千米处有一圆形敌楼名凤凰楼，高23米，直径16米，系用"砌 以砖石"的古老办法建成。正关八卦城易守难攻。

황야관장성 （韩文）

　　황야관장성（黃崖關長城）은 톈진（天津）시 지셴（薊縣）현의 북쪽에서 30km 떨어져 있으며, 천진 시내에서 100km 떨어져 있다. 황야관장성은 북제 천보 7 년（556）부터 건축하기 시작하여 명나라 융경（1567）년에 다시 벽돌로 수건하였다. 황야관장성은 험한 정상에 건설하였으며 담벽, 누각, 엄폐호, 수관, 돈대, 방어용 울타리 등 여러 가지 완벽한 방어시설을 구비하고 있다. 관 밖의 수천 미터 밖에 하나의 원형 적루가 있는데 평황루(鳳凰樓)라고 하며 높이 23m, 직경 16m 이고 중국 전통 방법으로 건설되었다. 정관 팔괘성은 방어가 쉽고 공격하기 매우 어려운 구조를 가지고 있다.

Huangyanguan （法文）

　　Huangyanguan está 30 kilómetros al norte del distrito de Jinxian, a más de 100 kilómetros de la ciudad de Tianjin. Se construyó en el séptimo año del reinado Tianbao (556) de la dinastía Qi del Norte y fue sometida a una importante restauración durante el reinado de Longqing, de la dinastía Ming. Está equipado con completas instalaciones de defensa, como atalayas, blindajes, cuarteles, almenas y parapetos. A pocos kilómetros metros del paso se levanta la torre del Fénix, una torre circular de 23 metros de alto y 16 metros de diámetro. Toda la ciudad del paso representa un dibujo de bagua (los Ocho Diagramas), forma que facilita la defensa y dificulta la conquista.

Huangya Pass （英文）

The Huangya Pass of the Great Wall stands 30 kilometres north of Jixian County and 100 kilometres from Tianjin. It was originally built in 556, the seventh year of the Tianbao reign of the Northern Qi Dynasty. In 1567, during the Longqing reign of the Ming Dynasty, the pass underwent major repairs and the wall was lined afresh with bricks.This section of the Great Wall with its watchtowers, battlements and barracks and moated defense works, is built on sharp mountain ridges. The entire structure looks majestic, formidable, precarious and elegant all at once. A round watchtower named phoenix Tower is 23 metres in height and 16 metres in diameter, and built of brick and stone in a traditional way. It stands several thousand metres outside the pass as a menacing sight in the eyes of invaders. South of the pass is China's first Great Wall museum.

Huangyuguan （德文）

Huangyayuan liegt 30 km nördlich vom Kreis Jixian und mehr als 100 km von der Stadt Tianjin entfernt. Dieser Abschnitt wurde 556 während der Nördlichen Qi-Dynastie gebaut und 1567 in der Ming-Zeit mit Ziegelsteinen ausgebaut. Die ganze Strecke liegt auf stilen Bergrücken und war mit zahlreichen Türmen und anderen Anlagen ein vollständiges Verteidigungssystem. Ein paar km entfernt ist ein runder Turm namens Phönixturm zu sehen. Er ist 23 m hoch und hat einen Durchmesser von 16 m . Der Hauptbau ist der Paß Baguacheng, der in alten Zeiten leicht zu verteidigen und schwer einzudringen war.

黄崖関長城 （日文）

黄崖関長城は、天津市薊県北部30キロの所に位置し、天津市から100キロあまり離れる。黄崖関長城は、北斉天保七年（556年）に建て始め、明代隆慶（1567）年間にまた大規模な改築が行った。長城の全部はきりとっいる岩壁につくられる。ここが堺台敵楼、町えんたい、関所煙台、町兵営等の各防備設備が揃え、関所の外から数千メートルの場所に丸型な敵楼を鳳凰楼と言い、高さ23メートル、直径16メートルで、「井戸や壁がれんがで造る」と言う古い方法を用いてつくりれた。正関はっけ城は守りやすく、攻めがたい。

Хуанъягуань （俄文）

Участок Великой Китайской стены Хуанъягуань находится в 30 км от уезда Цзисянь, более в 100 км от города Тяньцзинь. Он был построен в 556 году, потом с 1567 по 1572 год был перестроен. Данный участок Стены с дозорными башнями, зубцами, казармами протянулся на обрывистом горном переходе. Целое сооружение выглядит

великолепно и изыскано. Круглая дозорная башня, которая называется «Фэнхуанлоу», высотой 23 м., диаметром 16 м., была построена из кирпичей и каменей. Она стоит в несколько километров от заставы, и на глазах нападающих она является сильной преградой.

La Grande Muraille de Huangyayuan （西文）

Située à 30 km du district Jixian de Tianjin, la Grande Muraille de Huangyaguan se trouve à 100 km de Tianjin. La Grande Muraille de Huangyaguan est construite en 556 (7 ans de Tianbao des Qi du Nord), et restaurées en 1567 (de Longqing des Ming) et est revêtie de briques. Tous les murs sont construits sur des faîtes escarpées. Les installations de défense, comme fortins de guet, abrit, fumigènes, restes de caserne, sont très complets. Hors la passe, à des milliers de m, il dresse un fortin de guet. Appelé «Tour de Phénix», 23 m de haut, 16 m de diamètre,

assemblé de pièrre et de briques, d'un procédé antique. Le fortin de la passe est appelé «Cité de 8 Trigrammes», qui est facile à défendre mais difficile à attaquer.

Grande Muralgia di Huang'aiguan （意大利文）

La Grande Muraglia di Huang'aicheng si trova nella zone a distanza di 30 chilometri dalla cittadina di Jin a Tianjing, a distanza di oltre 100 chilometri da Tianjing. La Grande Muraglia di Huang'aiguan si inizieria a edificare nel 557 e il 1567. Tutta la grande Muraglia di Huang'aiguan sale serpeggiando sulla precipitosa spina del monte. Qui le installazioni per la difesa, ivi compresi le torre per la difesa dei nemici, sono complete. Fuori la fortezza nella zona a distanza di mila metri c'è una circolare torre, chinamandosi il palazzo di fenice, che è edificato con l'antica misura. La fortezza di fronte è facile di difendere e difficile di attaccare.

険峻的慕田峪箭扣長城
The precipitious Jiankou Great Wall at Mutianyu
慕田峪箭扣長城の険しい箭扣区間
험준한 무톈위젠커우장성
La Grande Muraille Jiankou à Mutianyu, connue pour sa topographie périlleuse
Die steile Jiankou-Strecke des Mauerabschnitts Mutianyu
La scoscesa muraglia Jiankou a Mutianyu
Стена «Цзянькоу» в Мутяньюй
La Gran Muralla de Jiankou en Mutianyu

气势雄伟的八达岭长城
The magnificent Badaling Great Wall
气势雄大の八達嶺長城
기세가 웅위로운 바다링장성
La Grande Muraille magnifique de Badaling
Die imposante Große Mauer in Badaling
La maestosa muraglia di Badaling
Великолелный участок Великой стены Бадалин
La Gran Muralla de Badaling

山海关

山海关在河北省秦皇岛市的东北，渤海湾的尽头。依山临海，地位险要，是万里长城东部的重要关口和战略要地。

"天下第一关"城楼为山海关东门，城楼东、南、北三面共开有箭窗68个，气势雄伟。山海关四门之外均有瓮城。历史上曾在此发生过很多战事。

Shanhai Pass（英文）

Located on the shore of the Bohai Bays in Qinhuangdao, Hebei Province, the Shanhai Pass forms the first pass at the eastern end of the Great Wall, hence its reputation as "the First Pass under Heaven".

The pass's east gate tower has 68 loopholes on the east, south and north walls. There are four watchtowers respectively built outside its four gates. The pass was fought over many times.

山海関（日文）

山海関は河北省秦皇岛市の東北、渤海湾の突き当たるところにある。山を背にして海に臨み、地勢が険阻な戦略的要地にある。万里の長城の東部における重要な関所である。

城楼の「天下第一関」は山海関の東門で、東、南と北の三面には合わせて68の射撃窓が開かれてある。4つの城門にも「甕城(関所を護る城)」がある。歴史上の多くの戦争はここで行われた。

산하이관 （韩文）

산하이관은 허베이성 친황다오시의 동북쪽, 발해만의 끝에 위치하여 있다. 뒤에는 산이 있고 앞에는 바다가 있으며 지세가 험준하다. 만리장성 동쪽 부분의 중요한 관문이며 전략적 요충지이다.

"천하제일관" 성루는 산하이관의 동문이고 성루의 동, 남, 북 세면에는 68개의 활을 쏘는 구멍이 있으며 기세가 웅위하다. 산하이관 4개 문밖에는 모두 옹성이 있다. 역사상 이곳에서 많은 전쟁이 발생하였다.

La passe Shanhaiguan （法文）

La passe Shanhaiguan est située au bord de la baie de Bohai au nord-est de Qinhuangdao dans la province du Hebei. Adossée à la montagne et baignée par la mer, elle occupe une position stratégique à l'extrémité est de la Grande Muraille.

La tour dressée sur la muraille au-dessus de la porte est de la passe Shanhaiguan porte l'inscription signifiant "la première passe sous le ciel" et les murs de ses trois côtés est, sud et nord comptent en tout 68 meurtrières. Les quatre portes de la passe sont respectivement protégées par une demi-lune. Dans le passé, beaucoup de batailles y ont eu lieu.

Shanhaiguan (Il passo Shanhai)（意大利文）

Shanhaiguan si trova a nord-est della città di Qinhuangdao, nella provincia dello Hebei, estremità del golfo di Bohai. Era il valico più importante della parte orientale della Grande Muraglia. La torre della città è la porta orientale del passo Shanhai. Sui muri orientale, meridionale e settentrionale della torre sono presenti 68 finestrelle da tiro. Fuori delle quattro porte del passo Shanhai si trovano cinta di muro. Questa fu una località che nel corso della storia assistette a numerose battaglie.

Шаньхайгуань （俄文）

Расположена к северо-западу от города Циньхуандао, на берегу Бохайского залива. Это важнейшая восточная застава Великой стены минской эпохи. Застава Шаньхайгуань представляет собой крепость прямоугольной формы с четырьмя воротами — восточными, южными, западными и северными. На восточной, южной и северной сторонах восточной башни заставы имеется 68 амбразурных щелей для стрельбы из лука.

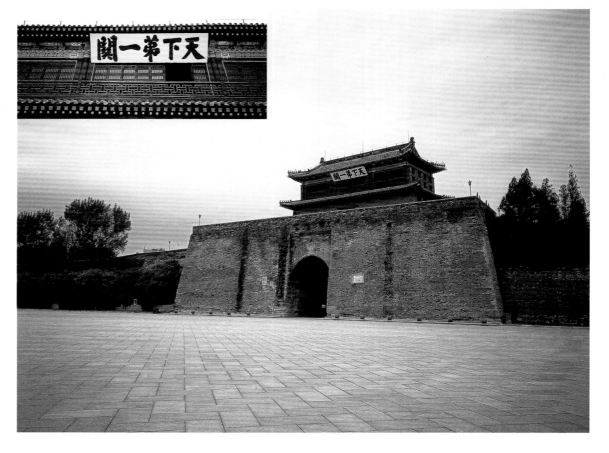

① 山海关关城全景
A view of Shanhai Pass
山海関関城全景
산하이관관성 전경
Panorama de la passe Shanhaiguan
Panorama der Guancheng-Festung des Shanhaiguan-Passes
Il panorama della muraglia Guancheng a Shanhaiguan
Панорама заставы Шаньхайгуань
Panorama de la Gran Muralla de Guancheng de Shanhaiguan

Der Shanhaiguan-Pass（德文）

Der Shanhaiguan-Pass liegt im Nordosten der Stadt Qinghuangdao der Provinz Hebei und grenzt im Norden an den Yanshan-Berg und im Süden an das Bohai-Meer. Er war eine schwer passierbare und daher strategisch wichtige Stelle.

Als der wichtigste Pass des Ostteils der Großen Mauer aus der Ming-Zeit hat Shanhaiguan vier Tortürme in vier Himmelsrichtungen. Am östlichen Torturm hängt eine horizontale Tafel mit der Inschrift „Der Erste Pass auf Erden". An der östlichen, südlichen und nördlichen Seite des Torturmes gibt es insgesamt 68 Schießfenster. Vor jedem Torturm wurde eine Schuztmauer gebaut. In der Geschichte geschahen hier viele Schlachten.

Paso Shanhaiguan.（西文）

Shanhaiguan, conocido también como Primer Paso Bajo el Cielo, se sitúa al noreste de la ciudad de Qinhuangdao, en la provincia de Hebei, a la orilla de la bahía Bohai. Apoyada en la montaña y bañada por el mar, su sede ocupa una posición clave, de ahí que se convirtiese en un importante y estratégico punto de acceso en el recorrido occidental de la Gran Muralla.

En la puerta occidental del paso se yergue un edificio solemne y majestuoso, a cuyos lados este, sur y norte dispone de un total de 68 ventanas para los arqueros. Fuera de las cuatro puertas del paso, se construyeron otras estructuras de refuerzo. Este lugar fue escenario de muchas batallas de guerras famosas.

山海关长城博物馆

山海关长城博物馆内展示了长城的历史渊源，建筑形制，人文历史，是中国以长城为专题的、较具规模的博物馆。

Shanhai Pass Great Wall Museum（英文）

One of the largest theme museums of its kind, the Shanhai Pass Great Wall Museum demonstrates the history, construction and historic relics of the Great Wall.

山海関長城博物館（日文）

長城にまつわる歴史、建築、人文などを専門とする博物館。中国でも規模がかなり大きい１つである。

산하이관장성박물관 （韩文）

산하이관장성박물관에서는 장성의 역사, 장성의 건축 형식, 장성의 인문역사 등을 전시한다. 장성을 테마로 하는 중국 박물관 중에서 규모가 비교적 큰 박물관이다.

Le Musée de la Grande Muraille de Shanhaiguan（法文）

Le Musée de la Grande Muraille de Shanhaiguan, spécialisé dans la présentation de l'histoire de la Grande Muraille, ses formes architecturales et l'histoire socioculturelle, est un musée d'une dimension assez grande en Chine avec la Grande Muraille pour thème.

Das Museum für die Große Mauer Shanhaiguan（德文）

Dieses Museum liegt in der Nähe des Shanghaiguan-Passes und ist ein Fachmuseum für die Geschichte der Großen Mauer Chinas.

Museo de la Gran Muralla del Paso Shanhaiguan.（西文）

El museo recoge de manera muy abarcadora la historia, estructura arquitectónica y cultura regional de la Gran Muralla.

Museo della Grande Muraglia di Shanhaiguan（意大利文）

Il Museo della Grande Muraglia di Shanhaiguan presenta la storia della Grande Muraglia, la sua architetura e la storia dei personaggi ad essa legati.

Музей Великой китайской стены в Шаньхайгуань（俄文）

Музей показывает историю, культуру и архитектуру Великой китайской стены. Является музеем с определенным масштабом в Китае, главной темой которого стала Великая китайская стена.

角山长城

角山长城位于山海关北3公里，角山主峰嵯峨，形似龙角。这里是长城自老龙头出海后西行向上的首段，故有"万里长城第一山"之称。

角山長城（日文）

山海関北3ｋｍの角山というところにある。角山の主峰は険しくて竜の角を思わせる。長城の城壁が海から伸び出るところ・老竜頭から西へ伸びた最初に出会った山であることから、昔から「万里長城第一の山」の称がある。

자오산(角山)장성（韩文）

자오산장성은 산하이관 북쪽에서 3km 떨어진 곳에 위치해 있는데 자오산 주봉이 우뚝 솟아 있는데 그 모양이 마치 용의 뿌리와 같다. 이곳은 장성이 라오룽터우(老龍頭)에서 바다에 이어지는 첫 구간으로 자고로부터 "만리장성제일산"으로 불리고 있다.

Jiaoshan Great Wall（英文）

Three kilometers north of the Shanhai Pass, the Jiaoshan Great Wall lies on the main peak of Jiaoshan Mountain, which looks like a dragon's horns. Starting from Laolongtou, the easternmost end of the Great Wall, this is the first section built on a mountaintop, hence its reputation "The First Mountain along the Great Wall."

La Gran Muralla de Jiaoshan （西文）

Tres kilómetros al norte del paso de Shanhaiguan aparece la montaña Jiaoshan, cuyo pico principal tiene la forma de un cuerno de dragón. Sobre esa elevación se extiende la primera sección del majestuoso baluarte defensivo, después de su punto de partida, en Laolongtou. Por esa razón fue bautizada como Primera Montaña de la Gran Muralla.

La Grande Muraille de Jiaoshan （法文）

La Grande Muraille de Jiaoshan est située à 3 kilomètres au nord de la passe Shanhaiguan. Le sommet des monts Jiaoshan, haut élevé, ressemble à une corne de dragon. Il s'agit de la première section de la Grande Muraille qui monte sur la montagne après sa sortie de la mer à Laolongtou, ce qui vaut aux monts Jiaoshan l'appellation de "Première montagne de la Grande Muraille".

La Grande Muraglia di Jiaoshan （意大利文）

La Grande Muraglia di Jiaoshan si trova a 3 chilometri a nord di Shanhaiguang. Il picco Jiaoshan somiglia a un corno di drago. Questo è il primo tratto della Grande Muraglia dopo il tratto della Muraglia che si affaccia sul mare, a Laolongtou, chiamato "Il primo monte sulla Grande Muraglia".

九门口水关长城
The Shuiguan Great Wall at Jiumenkou
九門口の水関長城
주먼커우수이관장성
La Grande Muraille de Jiumenkou, munie d'une passe sur l'eau
Der Mauerabschnitt Shuiguan in Jiumenkou
La muraglia Shuiguan a Jiumenkou
Участок Великой стены Шуйгуань в Цзюймэнькоу
La Gran Muralla de Shuiguan en Jiumenkou

Der Mauerabschnitt Jiaoshan（德文）

Dieser Mauerabschnitt liegt auf dem Jiaoshan-Berg, 3 km nördlich von dem Shanhaiguan-Pass entfernt. Der Jiaoshan-Berg rangt wie ein Drachenhorn an der Meeresküste empor und wird als der „Erste Berg der Großen Mauer" bezeichnet.

Участок Великой китайской стены Цзяошань（俄文）

Находится на 3 км от заставы Шаньхайгуань. Форма главного пика горы Цзяошань напоминает рог дракона. Является первым участком на горе после выхода из моря.

老龙头

从山海关东门往南，长城延伸直入海中，称为老龙头。城基伸入海中，之所以数百年海浪冲击仍巍然不动，是因为在海底安放很多铁锅，反扣海中，减小了海浪冲击的力量。这一科学的建筑办法曾被载入史册。在修建老龙头的同时，还建了城周0.5公里的宁海城，在城南垣建了一座高10米的澄海楼。

Old Dragon's Head（英文）

Lying south of the eastern entrance to Shanhai Pass, Laolongtou, or "Old Dragon's Head," is the easternmost end of the Great Wall, which stretches into the sea like a dragon drinking water, hence its name. Iron foundations help this point of the Wall to resist the pounding of the waves. In the vicinity are Ninghai Fortress, with a circumference of 500 meters, and the 10-meter-high Chenghai Tower to the south of the fortress.

라오룽터우 （韩文）

라오룽터우(老龍頭)는 장성이 산하이관의 동문에서 남쪽으로 바다까지 뻗어져 나간다고 하여 얻어진 이름이다. 성벽의 기초가 바다에 깊이 박혔는데 수백년동안 파도의 침식을 받고도 여전히 끄떡없다. 이것은 바다밑에 많은 철 가마솥를 거꾸로 박아넣어 파도의 충격을 약화 약화시켰기 때문이다. 이런 과학적인 건축방법은 이미 역사책에 기재되어 있다. 라오룽터우를 수건하는 동시 둘레가 0.5km인 닝하이(寧海)성을 구축하였으며 성남쪽 성벽에는 높이가 10m인 덩하이루(澄海樓)를 구축하였다.

Laolongtou （德文）

Es handelt sich dabei um einen Mauerabschnitt südlich des Shanhaiguan-Passes, der sich direkt bis zur Meeresküste schlängelt. Daher wird er Laolongtou (Kopf des alten Drachen) genannt. In der Umgebung gibt es viele Sehenswürdigkeiten wie die Ninghai-Festung und den 10 m hohen Chenghai-Turm.

Laolongtou （法文）

A partir de la porte est de la passe Shanhaiguan, la Grande Muraille se dirige vers le sud et entre finalement dans la mer. Ce tronçon de muraille est connu sous le nom de "Laolongtou". Malgré le battement des vagues depuis plusieurs siècles, la Grande Muraille reste inébranlable, c'est parce qu'on mit des marmites de fer de façon renversée sous la mer pour neutraliser le frappement des vagues. Ce procédé scientifique utilisé dans la construction de la Grande Muraille fut inscrit dans les annales. Lors des travaux, on édifia également la ville de Ninghai de 0,5 kilomètre de circonférence, sur le mur d'enceinte du côté sud de laquelle se dresse la tour Chenghai de 10 mètres de hauteur.

Laolongtou （意大利文）

A sud rispetto alla porta meridionale di Shanhaiguang, la sezione della Grande Muraglia che si getta verso il mare si chiama Laolongtou. Le fondamenta della struttura che si getta sul mare non sono in stato rovinoso nonostante sia continuamente colpito dalle onde da secoli. Per proteggere la struttura infatti, al momento della sua costruzione furono inserite nelle fondamenta delle lamine di ferro che hanno la funzione di ridurre la potenza dell'urto delle onde del mare. Questo tipo di rafforzamento è documentato da registrazioni storiche. Al tempo dell'edificazione di Laolongtou furono costruite anche la città di Haining che ha un perimetro di 500 metri e la torretta Denghai, alta 10 metri edificata a sud di Laolongtou.

Лаолунтоу (глава старого дракона) （俄文）

Часть стены из восточных ворот заставы, вдавшись в море, называется Лаолунтоу. Через много лет фундамент ее в море все таки крепок. Это потому что, под морем около фундамента были расставлены вверх дном многие железные котлы, которые могут ослабить силу волны. При строительстве Лаолунтоу строился городок Нинхай, периметр которого составляет в 0,5 км. На юге этого городка была построена башня Чэнхайлоу, высотой в 10 м.

Laolongtou (Cabeza del Viejo Dragón) （西文）

Desde la puerta occidental del paso Shanhaiguan, un tramo de la Muralla, llamado Laolongtou (Cabeza del Viejo Dragón), se extiende al sur y termina en el mar. La base de la edificación, sumergida bajo las aguas, pese a soportar durante centenares de años los golpes de las olas, se mantiene firme e intacta, según explican, gracias a las muchas ollas de hierro colocadas al revés en el fondo del mar, que protegen efectivamente el pedestal del embate. Al mismo tiempo que se levantó esta sección, se construyó en sus alrededores la ciudad de Ninghai y se erigió un edificio de 10 m. de alto en el sur de la localidad.

老竜頭（日文）

山海関東門を出た長城は、老竜頭というところで海に伸びていった。海に入っているその基礎部は、数百年にわたって波にさらされたが今も最初のままで堅固そのものである。その原因は築造当時に、波のさらされることを減らすために海底に伏せた多くの鍋にある。この方法は歴史の記録に残されている。老竜頭の建設に合わせて、周囲0.5kmの寧海城も建設され、城の南に高さ10mの澄海楼を建設した。

甘肃省山丹县附近的明万历年间修筑的长城遗址。

감숙성 산단현 부근의 명조 만력년에 부설된 장성유적

Ruins of the Great Wall built during the Wanli reign of the Ming Dynasty, at Shandan County, Gansu Province

Ruines de la Grande Muraille construite sous le règne Wanli de l'empereur Shenzong des Ming près du chef-lieu du district Shandan dans la province du Gansu

甘肃省山丹県付近にある明の万暦年間に築造した長城の遺跡

Ruine der Großen Mauer aus der Wanli-Regierungsperiode der Ming-Dynastie innerhalb des Kreises Shandan der Provinz Gansu

Resti della Grande Muraglia costruiti durante il periodo del regno dell'imperatore Wanli della dinastia Ming presso il distretto di Shandan nella provincia del Gansu

Ruina de la Gran Muralla al lado del distrito de Shandan de la provincia de Gansu, cuya construcción se data a los años Wanli de la dinastía Ming

Развалины Великой китайской стены, построенной при минском императоре Ванли (1563-1620) в уезде Шаньдань провинции Ганьсу

玉门关

汉代长城重要关隘，是西汉通往西域的交通门户之一，也是丝绸之路上的关隘。

Yumen Pass （英文）

As an important pass along the Great Wall, it served as a vital passageway toward the Western Region during the Western Han Dynasty. Merchant caravans along the Silk Road must cross here.

玉門関 （日文）

漢代長城の重要な関所で、後漢が西域に通じる大切な門戸の1つ。シルクロードの南、北、西の3線もここを通っていった。

위먼관 （韩文）

위먼관은 （玉門關） 한나라 장성의 중요한 관문으로 서한이 서역으로 나가는 관문의 하나이며 남,북 실크로드가 반드시 지나야 하는 관문이다

La passe de Yumen （法文）

Yumen, passe de la Grande Muraille des Han, était une des portes vers les Contrées de l'Ouest. Les branches sud et nord de la Route de la Soie passaient toutes les deux à travers cette passe.

Der Yumenguan-Pass （德文）

Der Yumenguan-Pass liegt in der Nähe der Kreisstadt Dunhuang der Provinz Gansu. In der Han-Dynastie war er eine wichtige Festung an der Seidenstraße und der Großen Mauer.

Yumenguan, il passo Yumen （意大利文）

Passo importante della muraglie dei Ming, quello di Yumen era una delle importanti vie d'accesso verso Occidente all'epoca della dinastia degli Han Occidentali, e fu un punto in cui si incrociavano gli itinerari Meridionale e Settentrionale dell'antica Via della Seta.

Юймэньгуань (Застава Яшмовых ворот) （俄文）

Был важным стратегическим пунктом Великой китайской стены в ханьской династии. Является одним из проходов из тогдашнего Китая на Запад. Южная, северная и западная части «великого шелкового пути» проходят Юймэньгуань.

Paso Yumen （西文）

Destacado punto estratégico en la Gran Muralla de Han, por ser la vía a través de la cual la dinastía Han del Oeste se comunicaba con los países occidentales y el único camino por el que pasaba la Ruta de la Seda.

阳关

阳关在玉门关之南，是汉长城重要关隘，也是丝绸之路必经之地。

Yangguan Pass （英文）

Located south of the Yumen Pass, this was an important pass on the Great Wall during the Han Dynasty (206BC-220AD), as well as a vital passageway along the Silk Road.

陽関 （日文）

玉門関の南にある。同じく漢代長城の重要な関所で、シルクロードの南北両線はここを通っていった。

양관 （韩文）

양관(陽關)은 위먼관 남쪽에 있는 한나라 장성의 중요한 관문이며 남, 북 실크로드가 반드시 지나야 하는 곳이다.

La passe Yangguan （法文）

Située au sud de la passe de Yumen, Yangquan était également une des importantes passes de la Grande Muraille des Han. Les branches sud et nord de la Route de la Soie passaient aussi à travers cette passe.

Der Yangguan-Pass （德文）

Der Yangguan-Pass liegt im Süden des Yumenguan-Passes. In der Han-Dynastie war er eine wichtige Festung an der Großen Mauer und an der Seidenstraße.

Il passo Yangguan （意大利文）

Situato a sud di Yumenguan, era anche un valico importante della muraglia della dinastia Han e un punto in cui si incrociavano i percorsi Meridionale e Settentrionale dell'antica Via della Seta.

Янгуань （俄文）

Расположен к югу Юймэньгуань. Тоже был важным стратегическим пунктом Великой китайской стены в ханьской династии. Южная и северная части «шелкового пути» проходят этот пункт.

Paso Yangguan （西文）

El paso se sitúa al sur del paso Yumen, fue también acceso importante de la Gran Muralla de Han y de la Ruta de la Seda.

"长城第一墩"位于甘肃嘉峪关以西。
The No.1 Mound of the Great Wall to the west of Jiayu Pass, Gansu Province
甘肃省嘉峪関西にある「長城第一の墩(のろし台)
간쑤성 자위관 서쪽에 있는 "장성 제일 돈대"
La première tour du feu d'alarme de la Grande Muraille à l'ouest de la passe Jiayuguan.
Der „Erste Signalturm" der Großen Mauer im Westen des Jiayuguan-Passes
"Il primo blocco della Grande Muraglia" si trova a ovest di Jiayuguan nella provincia del Gansu
Первая опора Великой китайской стены находится к западу заставы Цзяюйгуань провинции Ганьсу
"Primera columna de la Gran Muralla", situada al oeste del paso Jiayu, de la provincia de Gansu.

汉长城烽火台遗址
Remains of beacon towers of the Great Wall built during the Han Dynasty
漢代長城のろし台の跡地
한나라 장성 봉화대유적
Ruines d'une tour de vigie pour les feux d'alarme sur la Grande Muraille des Han
Signalturmruine der Großen Mauer aus der Han-Zeit
Resti della torretta del falò della muraglia edificata all'epoca della dinastia Han
Развалина сигнальной вышки ханьской Великой китайской стены
Ruina de la plataforma de alarma de fuego de la Gran Muralla de Han

汉长城遗址
Ruins of the Great Wall built during the Han Dynasty
漢代長城跡地
한나라 장성유적
Ruines de la Grande Muraille des Han
Ruine der Großen Mauer aus der Han-Zeit
Resti della muraglia edificata all'epoca della dinastia Han
Развалина Великой китайской стены в династии Хань
Ruina de la Gran Muralla de Han

嘉峪关

嘉峪关位于甘肃省河西走廊的西头，明代万里长城的西端即起于此。嘉峪关的南面是终年积雪的祁连山，长城直抵山下。关北是一片茫茫的戈壁滩，长城从嘉峪关向北伸展，再折向东穿过戈壁沙漠，翻山越岭直抵辽东，蜿蜒万里。

嘉峪关地处河西走廊之咽喉，地势险要，依山傍水，四面地域开阔，是建关守城的有利地形。嘉峪关也是现存长城千百座雄关中保存最完整的一座。

Jiayu Pass （英文）

The Jiayu Pass stands at the westernmost end of the Hexi Corridor in Gansu Province, and marks the western end of the Great Wall that was built during the Ming Dynasty. The snow-covered Qilian Mountains rise to the south of the pass, while a boundless desert spread to the north. Starting from the Jiayu Pass, the Great Wall stretches northward and then runs eastward for thousands of kilometers across deserts and mountains and plateaus to eastern Liaoning Province.

Jiayu Pass occupies a position of strategic importance along the Hexi Corridor. It is also the best-preserved among hundreds of passes along the Great Wall.

嘉峪関は甘肃省河西回廊の西端にあり、明代長城の西の起点である。南は年じゅう雪をいただいている祁連山で、長城はその裾まで続いていた。北はぼうぼうと広がるゴビ砂漠である。長城はまさにこの嘉峪関から北へ、また東のゴビ砂漠を通り過ぎ、山川を越えてえんえんと1万里の道のりをたどって、東の遼寧省東部に到着したのである。

嘉峪関は河西回廊という「咽喉となる地」にあり、地勢が険を極め視界が広く守るのにやさしい。中国に現存する1000あまりの関所の中でも、最も完全な形に保たれた関所の1つである。

자위관(嘉度關) （韩文）

자위관은 간쑤성 허시저우랑의 서쪽에 위치해 있으며 명나라 만리장성의 서쪽 끝이 여기서 시작되었다. 자위관의 남쪽은 사시장철 눈으로 덮혀 있는 치렌산(祁連山)이며 장성은 산아래로 쭉 뻗어 있다. 관문의 북쪽은 망망한 고비사막이고 장성은 자위관에서 북쪽으로 뻗었다가 다시 동쪽으로 굽어들어 사막을 관통하고 산을 넘고 영을 건너 구불구불 몇 만리를 지나 요동지구에 이른다.

자위관의 지리적 위치는 허시저우랑의 관건적인 입구이라고 할 수 있다. 자위관은 지세가 험준하고 산을 등지고 강을 끼고 있으며 사면이 광활하다. 관문을 구축하고 성을 수호하는 유리한 지형이다. 자위관은 지금 현존하고 있는 수천 개의 관문 중에서 가장 온전하게 보존된 관문의 하나이다.

La passe Jiayuguan （法文）

Située à l'extrême ouest du Corridor de Hexi dans la province du Gansu, la passe Jiayuguan marque l'extrémité ouest de la Grande Muraille des Ming. Au sud de cette passe ondulent les monts Qilian, couverts de neiges éternelles. La Grande Muraille se prolonge jusqu'au pied de cette montagne. Au nord de la passe s'étend l'immense désert de Gobi. La Grande Muraille se prolonge de la passe Jiayuguan vers le nord, puis tourne à l'est pour traverser le désert et se dirige ensuite jusqu'à l'Est du Liaoning en serpentant par monts et par vaux sur plus de 5 000 kilomètres.

Adossée à la montagne et baignée par une rivière, la passe Jiayuguan se trouve au point stratégique du Corridor de Hexi. Des quatre côtés, les terrains s'étendent à perte de vue. Cette topographie est très favorable à l'implantation d'une passe fortifiée. Jiayuguan est la passe la mieux conservée parmi tant d'autres subsistant sur la Grande Muraille.

Der Jiayuguan-Pass （德文）

Der Jiayuguan-Pass liegt am westlichen Rand des Hexi-Korridors der Provinz Gansu. Er bildet das westliche Ende der Großen Mauer aus der Ming-Zeit. Von hier aus schlängelt sich die Große Mauer ostwärts bis zum Osten der Provinz Liaoning. Im Süden des Passes liegt das schneebedeckte Qilian-Gebirge. An seinem Fuß sieht man noch viele Mauerabschnitte.

Dank seiner günstigen geografischen Lage war der Jiayuguan-Pass strategisch sehr wichtig. Heute ist er am vollständigsten erhalten.

Jiayuguan (il passo Jiayu) （意大利文）

Il passo Jiayu si trova nella parte occidentale del Corridoio Hexi, nella provincia del Gansu, all'estremità occidentale del tratto di muraglia edificato dai Ming. I monti innevati di Qilian e il deserto del Gobi sono situati rispettivamenta a sud e a nord del passo Jiayu. Partendo dal passo Jiayu, la Grande Muraglia si estende verso nord e dopo aver passato il deserto Gobi e le alte montagne giunge fino alla provincia del Liaoning, per una lunghezza di diecimila *li*.

Situato in un passo di difficile accesso del corridoio di Hexi, il passo di Jiayu era situato in una posizione geografica strategica che permetteva di avere un'ampia visuale dell'ambiente circostante. È in ottimo stato di conservazione.

Paso Jiayu （西文）

Enclavado en el punto oeste del Pasillo Hexi, en la provincia de Gansu, el paso Jiayu es también el extremo occidental de la Gran Muralla de Ming, que termina al pie de las montañas nevadas de la cordillera Qilian, al sur de esta vía. Parte de él se dirige al principio hacia el norte y luego dobla al este, después de atravesar el vasto desierto.

Dominando el cruce clave en el Pasillo Hexi, el paso se ubica en un terreno extendido y abierto, condición apropiada para levantar la fortaleza militar. Es también el paso mejor conservado entre los centenares que existen a lo largo de la Gran Muralla de Ming.

Застава Цзяюйгуань （俄文）

Расположена на западной оконечности коридора Хэси. Цзяюйгуань – западная оконечность отрезка Великой китайской стены, построенного в период династии Мин (1368-1644 гг.) . К югу ее возвышаются горы Циляньшань. К северу ее простирается пустыня Гоби.

Цзяюйгуань находится в ключевом пункте коридора Хэси. Она располагает благоприятной местностью для защиты города. К тому же, Цзяюйгуань – наиболее хорошо сохранившаяся застава Великой китайской стены.

图书在版编目（CIP）数据

长城／万博艺林图书有限公司编著. — 北京：外文出版
社，2008
ISBN 978-7-119-05344-8

Ⅰ.长… Ⅱ.万… Ⅲ.长城－画册 Ⅳ.K928.77-64
中国版本图书馆 CIP 数据核字（2008）第 053670 号

编　　著：万博艺林图书有限公司
责任编辑：兰佩瑾
摄　　影：张肇基　卞志武　谭　明
　　　　　吴健骅　武冀平　姜景余
　　　　　李　江

长　城

© 外文出版社
外文出版社出版
（中国北京百万庄大街 24 号）
邮政编码：100037
外文出版社网页：http://www.flp.com.cn
外文出版社电子邮件地址：info@flp.com.cn
　　　　　　　　　　　sales@flp.com.cn

2008 年 5 月(12 开)第 1 版
2013 年第 1 版第 3 次印刷
（英、汉、法、德、日、俄、意、西、韩）
ISBN 978-7-119-05344-8
06000 （平）